Landscape Design
@Canada

george lam / pace publishing ltd

WILL

editor : george lam (george@beisistudio.com)
design + colour edit : polly leung

pace publishing limited
17/f., north point asia-pac commercial centre,
10 north point road, hong kong
t: +852 28971688
f: +852 28972888
www.beisistudio.com
www.pacesource.com
pace@pacebase.com

isbn 978-962-7723-92-9
printed in china

CONTENTS

Parks, Gardens and Memorial

Residential

INTRODUCTION
Real Eguchi

REAL EGUCHI is a practising landscape architect and artist based in Toronto, Ontario, Canada. He holds degrees in architectural science, English literature and fine arts and received a Master of Landscape Architecture degree from the University of Guelph. Real is a member of the Ontario Association of Landscape Architects and the Canadian Society of Landscape Architects.

Real is the managing principal of Eguchi Associates Landscape Architects and a senior member of the collaborative studio bREAL inc., art + design. Examples of Eguchi Associates' current work include the design of a memorial park in Canada in collaboration with a Toronto artist, in honour of a former prime minister of Canada, and the master planning of islands of The World located off the coast of Jumeirah, Dubai, UAE. Some completed projects of Eguchi Associates are included in Landscape Design@XCanada.

It is an honour to present to you Landscape Design@Canada. As a practising Canadian landscape architect involved with the design of projects in Canada and abroad, this is a wonderful opportunity to reflect upon the state of the landscape architecture profession in Canada, as demonstrated in these projects that have been built in various regions of the country.

Landscape Design@Canada is one publication within a series dedicated to the promotion of excellence in landscape architecture in various countries throughout the world.

At first glance, it is immediately obvious that Pace Publishing Ltd. has made an extra effort to include projects in this publication that are representative of those created throughout Canada, within a wide range of sectors and of many different scales. Landscape Design@Canada focuses primarily on projects geared toward human use and enjoyment. The selected projects range from large planning initiatives to small urban gardens.

The Canadian Society of Landscape Architects and Town Planners (CSLA & TP) was founded in 1934. In the beginning, landscape architecture in Canada reflected both British and American influences combining Beaux Arts and neo-romantic styles. It was not until the 1960's that one might arguably suggest, a unique Canadian vision for landscape architecture emerged. At that time, the reference to Town Planners was dropped from the CSLA, the first two schools of landscape architecture were founded at the University of Toronto and at the Ontario Agricultural College (University of Guelph), and provincially based associations began to emerge. Currently there are ten provincial/ territorial based component associations under the unifying umbrella of the CSLA.

Landscape architecture in Canada is currently undergoing a tremendous period of growth, maturation and excitement. The revitalization of the waterfront in Toronto,

Ontario for example, is the focus of numerous local and international landscape architecture firms working on a multitude of coordinated projects. One of the projects is included in this book. These projects complement the architectural renaissance and the cultural revitalization of the city that is located on the north shoreline of Lake Ontario, one of the five Great Lakes that together constitute the largest body of freshwater in the world.

Canada is the second largest country in the world, (larger than China and the United States). Nature and the availability of natural resources play key roles in the psyche of Canadians and in the minds of landscape architects living and working in Canada. For decades, sustainability has been a central concern for landscape professionals who now play leading roles in our environmentally conscious culture, knitting together the social and ecological fabric within which Canadian lives can thrive.

As one peruses the projects featured in Landscape Design@Canada, it is an interesting exercise to try to discern commonalities amongst them. Is there a particular Canadian vernacular or style or a unique vision? Are there regional differences? To postulate, what defines Canadian landscape architectural projects is that they consistently embrace complex considerations with comprehensive responses resulting in high quality outcomes that are displayed in these implemented projects. Building codes, demanding safety requirements and rigorous municipal standards, help to ensure a high degree of quality and craftsmanship while challenging the creativity of landscape architects. As well, schools of landscape architecture in Canada, which are well recognized throughout the world, offer a close working relationship between practitioners and academics while ensuring that the most recent developments in research help to inform the latest design projects.

While it is an exciting period for landscape architecture in Canada, prospects for the future are even more so. In our interconnected world of high technology, virtual and multi-national design offices, Canadian landscape design talent is exported around the globe perhaps because of the comprehensive skills developed in response to the rigorous societal and academic standards demanded in Canada.

Technological advancements, such as computer modeling that has emerged as a dominant tool in the design process, without the proven overall skill of the landscape professional, do not guarantee successfully built projects. Admittedly, it is sometimes difficult to contemplate design quality when confronted with seductive and mesmerizing imagery that can be literally created overnight and could indeed be developed anywhere in the world.

The built project that one can examine, engage with, observe the use of and learn the most from, still remains the critical benchmark in the design process and upon which the success and quality of a design can be best determined. The projects included here are crafted out of tangible manufactured and living materials. They respond to their ecological and cultural context. They promote beauty and wellness in the lives of real people. They create a joyful sense of place and community and teach us to revere the planet earth, which sustains our lives. Through the compilation of these projects, this finely presented publication has successfully provided a glimpse of the art and science of landscape architecture as it is practised in Canada.

May Landscape Design@Canada encourage all readers to visit Canada and experience first-hand the wonderful projects that are presented amongst its pages.

Real Eguchi B.A., B. Tech. (Arch.), M.L.A., OALA, CSLA
September 11, 2007
Toronto, Ontario, Canada

Plazas and Streetscape

Toronto Central Waterfront 'Quay to the City'

West 8 + du Toit Allsopp Hillier

Born of the Toronto Central Waterfront Innovative Design Competition, Quay to the City was suggested by the jury to allow the public to imagine the proposed transformation of Queens Quay Boulevard by competition winners West 8 + DTAH. With the evolution of the masterplan now underway, the installation may prove critical in gaining public consensus and generating a mood of optimism for the work ahead.

'Quay to the City' is an experiment in reclaiming public space. For ten days in August 2006, the two eastbound lanes of Queens Quay Boulevard were closed and replaced with 2km of lawn, 12,000 red geraniums and an archway composed of 600 bicycles – the largest Toronto public art installation in recent memory. Quay to the City completed the Martin Goodman Bicycle Trail, allowing it to run uninterrupted from the East end Neighbourhoods to the West end, and pressed home the necessity for action on the waterfront as part of Toronto's urban renaissance. All materials were re-used for City of Toronto projects, including the lawn and all of the stone edging. The bikes, collected from City Works and the Toronto Police, were passed on to be auctioned or donated. On the last day, the public were invited to take home all of the geraniums as a keepsake.

Quay to the City allowed the Toronto public to see and feel the aspirations for the waterfront, and gave the design team and client the chance to interact with the target audience – from residents to merchants to tourists alike. Also, it revolutionized the planning process by giving people the chance to experience the design proposal and interact with it, rather than just review renderings and plans. This was also an exercise in information gathering – thousands of residents and tourists were surveyed during the event, and vehicular data collected in order to inform traffic simulations for the final design. It also gave the design team valuable insight into some of the constraints, approval processes and opportunities that will ultimately shape the final vision for Toronto's Central Waterfront.

→ Cyclists ride though the bicycle arch to celebrate the opening of the completed Martin Goodman Bicycle Trail.

↖ The bicycle arch attracted attention as one of the largest art installations in Toronto's history.

→ Close up of the bicycle 'Arc de Triomphe'.

← Cycling between the red geraniums and picnic lawn.

↖↖ Taking a piece of Quay to the City home - a little girl carrying pots of geraniums which were given to the general public on the last day of the event.

↖ City Staff look on as 12,000 geraniums are snapped up by the public in just a few hours.

← Harvesting geraniums - on the last day of Quay to the City, geraniums planted by the streetcar track were offered to the general public to take home.

← Events such as free kayak lessons were offered as part of Quay to the City.

↙ 100 muskoka chairs were placed along the water's edge, providing a relaxing place to sit on a hot day.

↓ Representatives of the three levels of government, the Honorable Michael D. Chong, Hon. David Caplan, and Mayor David Miller paint the lane stripe that completes the Martin Goodman Bicycle Trail.

client
Toronto Waterfront Revitalization Corporation
other key consultants
Civil / Traffic Engineering: Arup;
Industrial Design: David Dennis Design;
Construction Manager: Eastern Construction.
location
Toronto
completion
2006
photography
du Toit Allsopp Hillier

Green Necklace, City of North Vancouver

Tom Barratt Ltd / Dave Hutch, City of North Vancouver

The Green Necklace Communications + Marketing project was initiated by the City of North Vancouver to communicate a proposed 7km long urban greenway.

The Green Necklace is a 7km long urban greenway aiming to link the City of North Vancouver's park system in a continuous network of recreational and ecologically designed spaces to provide safe, alternative transportation routes through the City of North Vancouver.

The Landscape Architect assembled oversaw and coordinated a multidisciplinary team of graphic artists, 3D animation experts, planner and writer in the development of multi-media, multi disciplined communications and planning project.

The following communications components were developed: narrated digital flythrough of the 'Green Necklace, 3D animated detail, website development, marketing strategy, logo development and public consultation print media.

The Green Necklace website is: http://www.greennecklace.org

This project illustrates the role of the Landscape Architect adapting to and leading in new technologies and innovative communication techniques to further the understanding of the profession and its role in building communities.

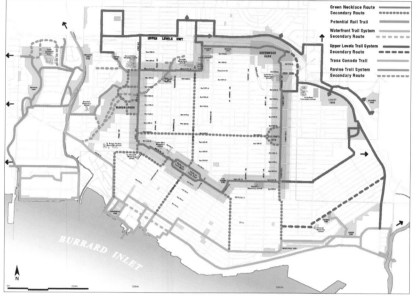

Legend:

Green Necklace Route
Secondary Route
Potential Rail Trail
Waterfront Trail System
Secondary Route
Upper Levels Trail System
Secondary Route
Trans Canada Trail
Ravine Trail System
Secondary Route

BURRARD INLET

↑ The Green Necklace is a 7km long multi-
← use trail that will form a continuous
loop around the centre of the City of
North Vancouver. It will link important
city parks, public spaces and natural
habitats, providing safe access for
pedestrians, people with mobility aides,
inline skaters and cyclists alike.

→ Pictures from 3D Animation.

↓ View of Green Necklace.

client
City of North Vancouver
other key consultants
Print media: Origin Design + Communications;
3D animation: Rob Tucker, Chinook Productions;
Website: Jeremy Burrows Creative;
Writing: Lance Berelowitz, The Sheltair Group.
location
North Vancouver, BC
completion
2005
photography
Dave Hutch

Sparks Street Mall
SWA Group

SWA Group provided conceptual design and design development services for the renovation of a pedestrian mall in downtown Ottawa. The new design for Sparks Street builds on a theme of tradition, elegance and distinction, while offering new opportunities for pedestrian and commercial use.

awards
Canadian Society of Landscape Architects (CSLA)
Merit Award

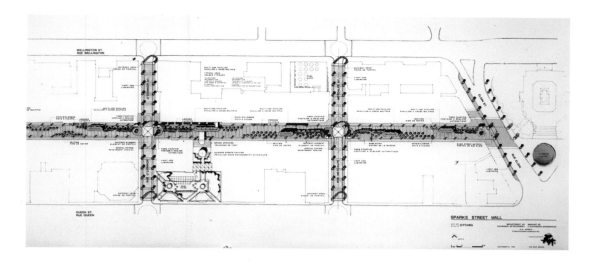

← Master landscape plan.

↓ Lighting fixtures designed by the Landscape Architect are reminiscent of old gas lighting. They provide a unifying element between contemporary buildings and period architecture along the mall..

← The new design for Sparks Street builds on a theme of tradition, elegance and distinction, while offering new opportunities for pedestrian and commercial use.

↗ Dramatic lighting features designed specifically for this site, borrow certain visual elements and materials from 19thC street lighting and give them a contemporary flair.

→ Materials were carefully selected to resonate with existing building facades.

→ Water features at every intersection provide visual connection along the several blocks of the mall.

↘ Seating areas are varied providing rest stops and meeting places all along the site.

↓ Historic Sparks Street was first pedestrian-only mall in Canada. The SWA design builds on the original mall plan with an updated and revitalized urban design plan.

← This historic redevelopment opens the mall to public events, adding seating, lighting, kiosks, water features and paving richness that stimulate community interest in the downtown area.

↑ Sparks Street features some of Ottawa's oldest historical buildings. The Landscape Architect used great care in the design and placement of architectural amenities on this historic street.

↖ The central roadway is transformed into a park plaza with pedestrian traffic moving freely along both sides.

↑ There are many opportunities to gather on the mall. Seat walls protect kiosk food court seating while providing additional seating.

client
City of Ottawa / Sparks Street Mall Board of Management
location
Ottawa, Ontario, Canada
other key consultants
Cecilia Paine & Associates, Associated Landscape Architect
photography
Tom Fox

Boulevard Honoré Mercier

WAA

The objective of this project was to redesign a major boulevard leading to Parliament Hill, in order to create an attractive and safe pedestrian environment where there used to be a major expressway entering the old town. During the 1960's and 70's, in the process of modernizing the city, numerous expressways and large boulevards were built in order to facilitate car movement and speed. Too often, the result was the creation of a bleak and sterile environment where cars occupied most of the space while pedestrians and nature were left out. Under strong leadership of the Mayor of the city of Quebec and the CCNQ, numerous projects in this UNESCO world heritage city where undertaken to make the city more convivial to pedestrians and thus offer a better living environment. Honoré Mercier Rehabilitation is a key element in these undertakings.

In a rather small space, and preserving the presence of car circulation, the rehabilitation plan proposed to add festive sculptural elements, trees, shrubs and other green spaces and floral displays, in addition to wider sidewalks in order to transform and enliven a formerly bleak, dangerous and unpleasant thoroughfare. The results are striking! Large esplanade type sidewalks and paved car intersections create the setting for a public realm where pedestrians are welcomed and cars are forced to slow down. The addition of public art, lighting and plantings create a welcoming effect in the Capital known for its culture, beauty, and unique natural environment. While providing the necessary car space, this main entrance from the expressway is now a redefined, safe and enjoyable public space for visitors and citizen alike. The design brought new hotels and other businesses to an area that was not previously seen as a key investment environment. The project has received numerous awards and design recognition.

← View looking down towards the North from the central median.

↓ The central median towards the connection with the Expressway at the north end of the Boulebard.

↖ A fast moving car lane gave way to a small urban plaza for people to enjoy city life and the unique views offered towards the north.

↑ Looking down towards the north, the street is now a pleasing green oasis with many trees, plants, and artwork.

↓ Seen from the sidewalks, the street is inviting and green making this a people environment rather than a car thoroughfare. The green plateaus are visible in the back.

← The steep slope offers green plateaus where various plants and grass offer an inviting entrance to the historical city and parliament buildings.

client
National Capital Commission of Quebec (CCNQ)
and City of Quebec

other key consultants
Architecture de paysage. Urbanisme. Design
urbain
André Plante – Architecte paysagiste
Ville de Québec
Service de l'aménagement du territoire.
Division du design, de l'architecture et du
patrimoine de la Ville de Québec
Michel Dallaire - Michel Dallaire Design Industriel
Paul Béliveau - Artiste
Gilles Arpin - Éclairage public – Concepteur
Lumière
BPR, GÉNIVAR, et TECSULT - Génie

location
Québec, Québec

completion
2003

Marinaside Crescent
SWA Group

SWA provided urban design and overall conceptual landscape architectural design for this mixed-use project including condominium buildings with shops, restaurants and storefronts at street level, a waterfront promenade, a marina, parks and inner building courtyards, and pedestrian-oriented pathways linking the Marinaside Crescent Road and surrounding streets. The design goals included view preservation, pedestrian access to the water, vehicular and non-vehicular movement throughout the site, privacy and livability.

↑ Marina side walkways form the waterfront edge of several linked parkways in this ocean front community development.

→ Master landscape plan.

← Broad upper tree-lined walkways provide easy access to the water free of any competition from vehicular traffic.

↓ Inner courtyards are designed as pocket parks both for residents and visitors to the waterfront.

✓ Paved bicycle paths are separated from pedestrian walkways along the water.

↑↑ Park-like corridors between buildings provide opportunities for commissioned artists to exhibit public sculpture.

↑ Courtyards are centered on parterre gardens surrounding a central fountain.

↗ An on-structure koi pond provides visual interest for people as they meander along pathways through the site.

↑   European-style paving patterns designate walkways through the use of varied paving patterns in the roadway itself.

↗   Perennials and ornamental grasses are used to screen residences from walkway traffic and to add visual interest to walls and walkways.

→   Two-way traffic is confined to the upper parkway. By design, roadways are tree-lined throughout the neighborhood.

↓   Highrise multi-family residences are fronted by street level shops and service centers.

← People of all ages walk and bicycle along the street. Again, paving designates special interest or direction, designating each storefront through change in pattern.

→ Several restaurants invite visitors to dine along the way.

→→ Sidewalk seating provides streetside interest for strollers and diners alike.

↘ The project features a shopping district that includes grocery stores, banks and coffee shops.

client
Concord Pacific Development Corp.
location
Vancouver, British Columbia
other key consultants
James KM Cheng, Architects, Ltd.
photography
Tom Fox

Hanover Heritage Square
Eguchi Associates Landscape Architects

Enhancing Civic Wellness and Beauty

Hanover Heritage Square is the central outdoor civic space for the Town of Hanover, Ontario, a town with a population of 7000. The Square is located on the commercial main street of the Town and across from the Town's primary civic facilities.

The 0.6 hectare property was originally the site of the Knechtel Furniture Factory, the key company in the Town's development that also led the Town's illustrious, furniture manufacturing industry and resulted in its past international recognition as 'The Furniture Capital of Canada'. The factory building was destroyed in a fire and demolished in the 1980's after nine decades of the factory's considerable main street presence.

The Square is a unique, visual and symbolic landmark that enhances civic pride and reconfirms the collective memory of the citizens of Hanover. It is a metaphor for the aspirations of the community and a legacy for the future citizen's of the Town of Hanover. The Square is evolving as an essential intervention within the social and environmental fabric of the Town. It serves as a crucial instrument that structures social interaction while enhancing the quality of the public realm.

The Square includes a series of contrasting yet complementary 'places' that together encourage meaningful and varied activity and various opportunities for self-revelation within the ongoing renewal of Hanover's cultural continuum. These places, or 'living' rooms for gathering and community building, are strongly linked to the Town's historic Clock Tower and Civic Centre across the street and to the adjacent Town Mural. Together they form an integrated civic precinct. Linkages are also provided to the past, through heritage recognition, as well as to the future with intentional design flexibility for the input of future generations and initiatives. The Square, a combined park and plaza, is a vibrant, passive recreational open space, a central destination node to complement the existing dynamic of the Town's main street.

awards
*2005 Regional Citation Award, Canadian Society of
  Landscape Architects;
EDCO 2003 Ontario Economic Development Award.*

→ Site Plan.

↓ Aerial View of Hanover Heritage Square looking south-west toward the Town's Civic Centre, Library, Clock Tower and Mural.

Pedestrian circulation within the site is enhanced with two major walkways that intersect at the Civic Plaza.

The diagonal line of the Heritage Promenade, a wood boardwalk combined with distressed concrete pavers, bisects the entire site as a visually simple yet dynamic, linear datum to enhance leisurely strolls and formal processions through the site. All primary spaces on the site are 'attached' to the promenade to create a coherent yet complex landmark and visitor experience.

The graceful curve of the West Walk embraces the Green Common and provides access from the adjacent municipal parking lot. The Celebration Tree, Picea glauca, sits prominently on the Celebration Knoll and serves as a visual focal point along the West Walk and as a feature for orientation and delight from all directions.

Buck's Crossing is a symbolic, third walkway that crosses the street from the Clock Tower and terminates within the Civic Plaza. (completed after the photo was taken) As the founder of Hanover, Abraham Buck is credited with settling at the Saugeen River, creating a bridge over the river and establishing Buck's Crossing that would later become the Town of Hanover.

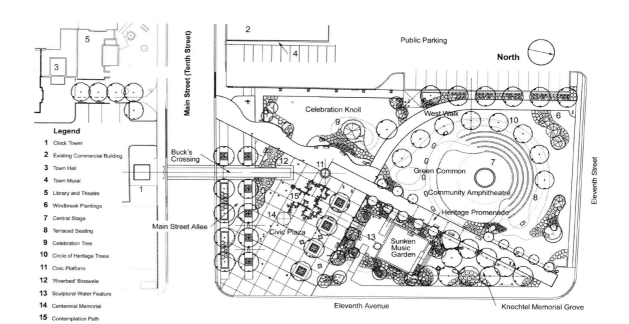

Legend

1 Clock Tower
2 Existing Commercial Building
3 Town Hall
4 Town Mural
5 Library and Theatre
6 Windbreak Plantings
7 Central Stage
8 Terraced Seating
9 Celebration Tree
10 Circle of Heritage Trees
11 Civic Platform
12 'Riverbed' Bioswale
13 Sculptural Water Feature
14 Centennial Memorial
15 Contemplation Path

↖ The Civic Plaza is the ceremonial place of active convergence. The circular Civic Platform mimics the larger Central Stage of the Community Amphitheatre. The Contemplation Path, dubbed the 'Walk of Distinction', chronologically orders the names of prominent figures in Hanover's history as it weaves its way around the plaza. The path terminates at the Centennial Memorial Marker and Garden. (not yet installed in this photo) Beyond the memorial, a plan was formulated for the path to continue for the next 100 years. In contrast to the ordered walk, the names of all the Mayors in Hanover's history have been engraved, each individually, on one recognition paving stone. The pavers are scattered randomly throughout the plaza to add a sense of mystery and discovery for school groups and others intrigued with Hanover's heritage.

↑ The Knechtel Memorial Grove continues to develop as a naturalistic, quiet woodlot for contemplative thought. It is a symbol of the larger, less ordered, natural context that was critical to the development of the wood furniture industry. Fraxinus americana 'Autumn Purple' provides a shady, green sitting area that turns to a warm, reddish/purple autumn hue. Engineered wood fibre, serves as a cost-effective gentle walking surface that binds together for reduced maintenance.

An aluminum display case houses a wood medallion (Knechtel Furniture Factory logo) carved by a local craftsman, and the factory steam whistle that was heard daily throughout the Town for decades while the factory was in operation.

↗ Plantings serve as visual scrims, articulating views within the Music Garden's growing, plant matrix.

↘ The Community Amphitheatre and Green Common together form a circle, a symbol of unity and a place for community gathering and celebration. This area also serves as a stormwater detention area and the circular lawn is carefully graded to accommodate an intimate, natural ice rink in the winter to further encourage a sense of civic togetherness.

↓ Local, sparkling pink granite was sculpted to form a water feature in the form of an assembly of musical instruments that is located in the Music Garden. A simple, low-maintenance, mechanical system was used and the water enhances sensory and interactive delight.

← The double row of Tilia cordata, with its yellow fall colour, is maturing as the dense canopy of the formal and linear Main Street Allee.

↙ This view of the Sunken Music Garden toward the historic Clock Tower, Town Hall and Library, reveals the success of the Civic Precinct configuration that the project has established. The dynamic order of the Music Garden, included in the project in recognition of Hanover's illustrious musical heritage, is established by the layout based on the Golden Section.

client
Town of Hanover
project team - eguchi associates
Principal-in-Charge, Real Eguchi, B.A., B.Tech. (Arch.), M.L.Arch., OALA, CSLA
Design Principal, Barbara Flanagan-Eguchi, B.L.Arch., OALA, CSLA
Team Members: Ken Nice, Tad Ukleja.
other key consultants
Architectural Heritage Consultant: Robert Greenberg;
Town of Hanover Historian: Alred Morrow;
Lighting Design: Lightstudio Inc.;
Civil and Structural Engineer: George A. Davis and Associates Limited;
Water Feature Mechanical Design: The Waterworx Company.
location
Hanover, Ontario
completion
2004
photography
bREAL Art + Design

Parliament Hill

Under the authority of the National Capital Commission, we were commissioned to undertake the preparation of a rehabilitation plan for the entire Parliament district. The planning strategy was accepted and it led to an ambitious program to rehabilitate the core of the area, and eventually several major historical and cultural sites in the area. The first phase of the project encompassed the park and esplanade facing the Parliament Building. Established more than one hundred years ago, the site was in great disrepair. Following an in depth historical study and several consultations, a master plan was adopted and implemented. It features the rehabilitation of the circular round about using high quality materials, such as granite, creating the feeling of a public esplanade that can support cultural activities and improvised gatherings. The existing car circulation was redesigned to meet new standards and allow for public touring buses. In order to take full advantage of the most photographed building in the city, a large floral planting in shades of blue with white accents was added (to recall the provincial flag), along with urban furniture and flagpoles. Special areas for official commemoration were integrated, and old monuments were restored and relocated in a comprehensive way. The space is both official and festive as it is the centre of summer festivities and the Quebec winter carnival.

The project is distinguished by its simplicity, through the subtle sense of openness and enclosure created by the double rows of trees, the quality of its materials, and its construction details.

↓ View of the entrance mall and roundabout in front of the Parliament.

– 51 –

↖ Ground view of the roundabout and commemorative wall. The wall is designed to represent the "glacis" mounds that used to protect the Fortification of the City.

↗ A viewing platform at the edge of the parliament grounds overlooking in one direction the Parliament and in the other the "Fortified" city of Quebec.

→ Tree covered sidewalks and commemoration are part of the public realm.

← Looking towards the Parliament building.

client
National Capital Commission of Quebec,
City of Quebec
other key consultants
Gauthier, Guité, Daoust, Lestage et Associés
location
Québec, Québec
completion
1999

International Business District, Montreal

WAA

This new urban space is the "Quartier International de Montréal", known as Montreal International District. As a large-scale urban development project, the Quartier International aims to showcase and promote Montréal's international role. The Quartier International builds upon a modern, prestigious, and exclusive urban design providing a unique living environment in the very heart of Montréal's downtown area. This project, which represents an investment of over $60 million, is the result of an original partnership between the private and public sectors.

From an urban area made dysfunctional by a section of the Ville-Marie expressway has emerged a modern, prestigious and lively environment. The Quartier International is, first and foremost, an exceptional urban development project whose goal is to create a new urban space in the heart of the downtown area. By putting quality first, the Quartier International has become a true showcase of Québec know-how.

This concern for a quality urban development is reflected in the redesign of the urban fabric through the use of unique street furniture, public art, and a theatrical use of lighting. In this project, every effort is made to create a congenial space and a friendly environment for the people circulating, working in, or visiting the Quartier International.

This prestigious urban development was realized by creating and redesigning public spaces covering the Ville-Marie expressway (such as Place Jean-Paul Riopelle and Victoria Square). This was accomplished by linking the protected pedestrian network, as well as carrying out continuous urban interventions on the sector's main circulation axis. Furniture, lighting, paving and all other aspects reflect quality in the design and construction. The project has won more than 12 awards over the last few years making it a leading example of excellent planning and design.

↖ The new Square Victoria, a modern plaza in the heart of the
old city.

↑ Place Riopelle

↓ Plan of Place Riopelle, with the famous sculpture design
by Riopelle and relocated here in the heart of the Quartier
International de Montreal.

← In the foreground, the new square with its modern fountain
and distinctive furniture, in the background the rehabilitated
old Square Victoria.

client
City of Montreal in partnership and
La Corporation Montréal international
other key consultants
Daoust Lestage Inc., Provencher Roy and
associates
Architects in joint venture, Architecture and Urban
Design
location
Québec, Québec
completion
2004

Burnaby Civic Square and Library
SWA Group

Urban design plan and development for this three-building complex that includes a library and civic space for the Metrotown area of the city of Burnaby. The design features a civic lawn and parterre garden, fountains, and an allée of honey locust trees. The library and most of the central garden space are built over a two-level underground parking structure. To avoid the restrictions on tree use placed on a rooftop landscape, SWA planted the two rows of honey locust trees in tree wells suspended in the garage. The complex provides an opportunity to express public significance to the growing city.

↑   The landscape architect designed the glass and steel bandshell to evoke the light and pattern of garden pavilions of an earlier time.

↓   SWA provided an urban design plan and development for this complex that includes a library and civic space.

↘   Landscape master Plan of the new civic plaza in the heart of Burnaby, Ontario, Canada.

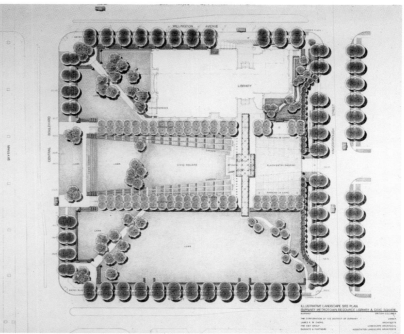

↖ The fountain lighting creates atmosphere for nighttime events.

↑ The forced perspective focusing on the civic "bandshell" and flanking colonnades, and the siting and character of the library building all combine to create a "sense of place" for the City.

→ Over 45 civic and community events now currently held at the civic square each year including Art Fairs, concerts, book drives and Civic Ceremonies. On a da to day basis, it is an outdoor living space for the city.

← In the parterre garden, as the planting beds of lawn, hedge, seasonal color and fountains extend from east to west, their shape and plantings modulate, creating added interest and richness to the ground plane.

←← An elevator to the garage and a music storage equipment room are accommodated in the adjoining two glass block structures.

↑ The design features a civic lawn and parterre garden.

← The plaza is built completely on-structure, lawn and trees are thrive in a shallow planting clearance arrangement above lower level amenities.

← View toward Sky Train, grand terrace and stair. At the far end of the lawn, a wide expanse of ceremonial stairs affords maximum access to the site as well as providing theater-type seating for events.

↓ Paving detail at children's garden. Multi-colored tile evokes a colorful sea of animals to accentuate the playfulness of this space.

↙ Burnaby is a neighboring district of Vancouver, British Columbia. The new civic center project creates a civic focus for that community, expressing the pride of a growing city.

client
Corporation of District of Burnaby
location
Burnaby, British Columbia
other key consultants
James KM Cheng, Architects, Ltd.
photography
Tom Fox

Waterfront Centre
SWA Group

SWA provided landscape design for the plaza and garden at Waterfront Centre, the major open space for Vancouver's dynamic western waterfront. The sunken garden protects urban workers, tourists and conventioneers from the coastal wind and gives separation from the major street at the edge of the bay. The plaza and garden is at the end of the pedestrian route from Vancouver's business center. It features a water element that masks street noise to provide a quiet refuge from the activity that surrounds it.

↑   Cascading water masks street noise and provides an atmosphere of repose in the heart of the city.

↘   Green terraces form an amphitheater, providing an outdoor venue for public events in the city.

↓   Strength of design is apparent in all aspects of the plaza. Line intervals, balance of form and proportion provide a visual rhythm reflected in every detail.

↑ Dramatic water elements carry the sound of water throughout the site.

↘ By design, this sunken garden plaza is sheltered from north coastal winds, gathering the warmth of the sun to this unique location in the urban cityscape.

↓ The gracious sweep of the entry staircase modulates the transition from street to garden plaza.

The plaza and garden is at the end of the pedestrian route from Vancouver's business center.

The sound of water welcomes busy pedestrians visitors to the garden on the street level.

The spiral form of the entry fountain is repeated in the inverse form of the main fountain that carries the water down from street level to the plaza..

client
Marathon Realty Company Ltd.
location
Vancouver, British Columbia
photography
Tom Fox

Institutional and Educational

Terrence Donnelly Center for Cellular and Biomolecular Research

Diana Gerrard Landscape Architecture
with
Behnisch Architekten
architectsAlliance

Terrence Donnelly Center for Cellular and Biomolecular Research (TDCCBR) is Canada's foremost human genome research center, home to 400 specialists in genetics and disease research. A collaborative, interdisciplinary research center, TDCCBR is functional, highly flexible, and technologically advanced. Formerly used as a parking area, the narrow building site is wedged between two historic buildings, and makes symbolic and physical connections uniting the academic community, the medical community, and the general public.

The primary components of the landscape are the Wintergarden in the west side of the building and the stair and ramp from the street that forms a new gateway to the campus. The Wintergarden is planted simply with two species: Giant Grey Bamboo and Lirope Grass. The intent is a temperate landscape that mediates between TDCCBR and the historic Rosebrugh building and does not compete with all of the architectural activity.

On the upper floors of the building are four smaller gardens, again planted with two temperate species: Black Olive and Creeping Fig. These small gardens, like the Wintergarden, provide both physical and psychological amenity.

Outside is a grove of birch. Similar in tone and form to the bamboo inside, the birches unite the indoors and out-of-doors and perform the role of a shaded oasis. Functionally, the birches operate similarly to the bamboo as mediators between TDCCBR and the historic Rosebrugh and Fitzgerald buildings.

The stair and ramp from the street are captured within the birch grove. The scale of these elements brings the street onto the site and symbolically replaces the street that was removed. The selection of black granite for the ramp and stair integrates them into the fabric of the University as a whole.

Further integrating the TDCCBR with the University, the landscape provides enhanced pedestrian corridors that have been created for all of the buildings involved.

awards
2006 International Award, The Royal Institute of
British Architects (RIBA);
2006 Award of Excellence, Ontario Association of
Architects (OAA);
2007 Architectural Record/BusinessWeek Award.

↑   The use of granite on the exterior forecourt continues into the building, for an indoor-outdoor sensibility.

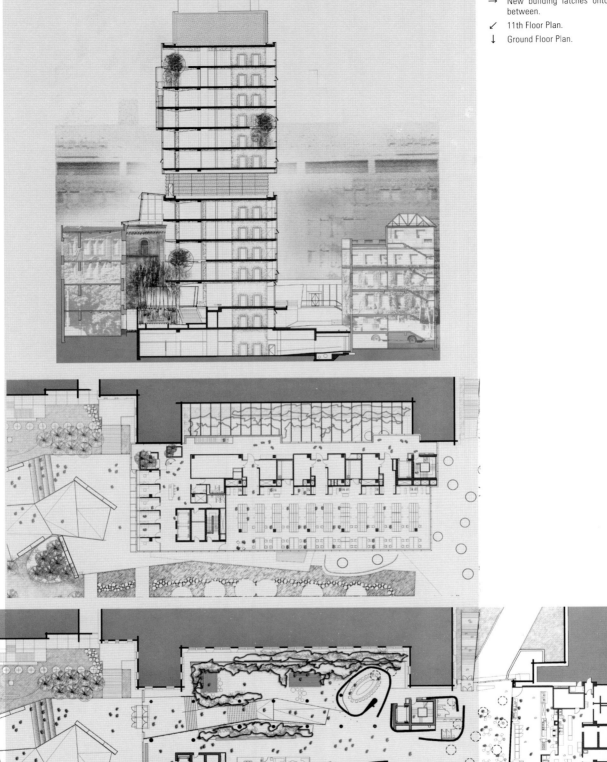

← Section showing wintergarden and upper gardens.
→ New building latches onto old, with garden in between.
↙ 11th Floor Plan.
↓ Ground Floor Plan.

©Ben Rahn

↑   Bountiful natural light encourages growth and maintenance of interior gardens.

→   Indoor gardens are irrigated and drained as part of the building's storm-water reclamation system.

©Tom Arban

↖ The gardens throughout the facility act as lounges, creating ideal spaces for relaxation and informal meetings.

↑ Multi-layers of gardens and open light wells let natural light penetrate the building.

↘ The use of granite on the exterior forecourt continues into the building, for an indoor-outdoor sensibility.

↓ An interior deck ideal for quiet respite is lined with 45-foot-high bamboo trees and Liriope grass.

← Gardens outside of researchers' offices.

©Tom Arban

©Tom Arban

client
University of Toronto
location
Toronto, Ontario
completion
November 2005
photography
Tom Arban & Ben Rahn

University of Ontario Institute of Technology

du Toit Allsopp Hillier

The University Campus is located in Durham County, an hour east of Toronto and adjacent to the Oshawa Creek Ravine. Situated in the heart of Canada's automotive industry, the university is keen to be a flagship for technological excellence.

The guiding principle of the design was to seamlessly integrate a new university within the site an existing technical college campus. Arranged around a new central quadrangle, the campus landscape was intended to be a cutting-edge, green campus landscape that would visibly demonstrate a commitment to sustainable design. Within this framework, the movement of rainwater – from its source on rooftops and parking lots, to its release in Oshawa Creek or re-use in irrigation – organizes and articulates the landscape design. The resulting framework defines the campus structure and character, inspiring the visual and functional components of the exterior spaces. Stepped linear wetlands, bio-swales and storm ponds complete with waterside spouts and scuppers, articulate the site to engage, amuse and inform students and visitors.

With the mission of delivering an environmentally responsible campus

awards
*2006 Honour Award for Excellence in Planning,
 Society for College and University Planning;
2005 Regional Honours Award, Canadian Society of
 Landscape Architects.*

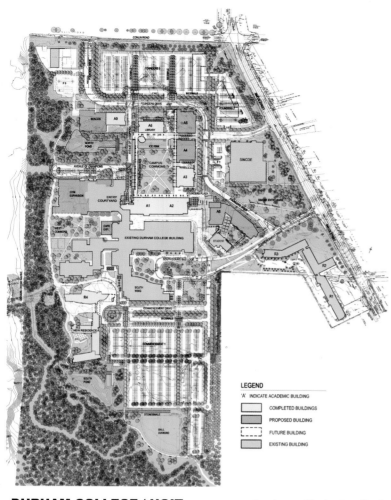

DURHAM COLLEGE / UOIT   Landscape Masterplan -Final

du Toit Allsopp Hillier

LEGEND

'A'   INDICATE ACADEMIC BUILDING

COMPLETED BUILDINGS

PROPOSED BUILDING

FUTURE BUILDING

EXISTING BUILDING

↑   Plan.

↗   Aerial view with South Pond and new residence building in foreground, along with existing ball diamond. Existing Durham College building centre page, new university quadrangle and storm pond to north of existing college.

↘   The fire access ramp viewed from the Entry Courtyard. The Stepped linear wetland adjacent to the University Quadrangle (Campus Commons) is on the right.

development, the university core was designed to receive a Borehole Thermal Energy System. Situated in the heart of the campus below the central quadrangle, it provides temperature control for the main academic buildings. A continuous service tunnel links all of the core buildings, and their roof water is fed into a 250,000-litre cistern to be used for irrigation of the central planted spaces.

The integration of sustainable design principles reinforces the University's commitment to learning, teaching and professional practice in a technologically progressive environment. The goal is a campus framework that allows for flexible expansion of the new university. In future phases, additional residences will help transform the campus from a commuter college to a mixed-use institutional focus for the larger community.

Sustainable design aside, the campus was also intended to embody the more emotive and tactile qualities of a well-loved campus. The scale, spatial qualities and materials were carefully studied to ensure that the new University would become a nurturing and proud home to future generations of staff and students.

↑   The Reflecting Pool / Ice Rink and library at the north end of the Campus Commons.

↘   View north from the Entry Courtyard.

↓   The Campus Commons, library, west colonnade and main academic buildings viewed from the Entry Courtyard.

↑↑ The south pond forebay, weir wall and lookout, viewed from the south bank in fall of 2005.

↑ View along the west colonnade towards the library, with the Campus Commons on the right. The trench drain is connected through wall scuppers to the linear wetland.

↘↘ Stone bench and grass planting in front of academic building.

↘ Metal scuppers spilling water to the south pond.

↓ The north pond forebay, weir wall and lookout. The west colonnade and main academic buildings are in the background.

↑ View from the weir wall towards the Oshawa Creek Ravine, showing the waterside deck and pedestrian bridge.

↗ View from the south pond lookout towards the weir wall and pond forebay.

↓ View of north pond framed by the main academic buildings and Campus Commons.

↖ The south pond pedestrian bridge viewed from the pond side.

↑ View east towards the south pond pedestrian bridge, where the stone drainage swale enters the south pond.

↓ View south along stone drainage swale adjacent to the south (Commencement) parking lots.

client
Province of Ontario / Durham College UOIT
other key consultants
Architects: Diamond and Schmitt Architects Inc.;
Landscape Ecologists: Schollen and Company;
Civil Engineering: TSH;
Electrical Engineering: Carinci Burt Rogers;
Industrial Design: David Dennis Design.
location
Oshawa Ontario
completion
2005 / ongoing
photography
du Toit Allsopp Hillier

Lester B. Pearson Garden for Peace and Understanding

PMA Landscape Architects Ltd.

Lester B. Pearson served as the fourteenth Prime Minister of Canada and is recognized for his international and national presence and roles, as well as that at Victoria University where he studied and later on, became Chancellor. This garden commemorates his life and the peace towards which he worked, and was made a Nobel Laureate in 1957.

The Lester B. Pearson Garden for Peace and Understanding acts as an island of serenity and inspiration within Victoria University, in the University of Toronto campus. The lush vegetation combined with the soft sound of the waterfall offer students, staff, faculty, and the general public, seclusion from the context found beyond the borders of the campus and within Toronto's metropolitan downtown.

The concept of the garden aims at to accentuate the differences among the variety of elements of the site. There is an overall stillness, quietness, and solidity in the garden. Elements include the calm reflective pool against the waterfall; the smooth concrete slabs versus the craggy stone; the enclosure vis-à-vis the open chaos of Queen's Park Crescent; and the piercing white stone amongst the multitude of colors of vegetation. There is a collective symbolic experience within the garden. Contrasting elements stimulate the senses and calm the emotions, where a retreat is sought on this campus of higher education.

PMA's role in this project included the overall design, to project management and construction supervision. The project involved a high-degree of design detailing and co-ordination with specialized individuals in stone masonry, metal work, bronze work, water works, and horticulture. The opening of the garden ceremoniously unveiled the custom-made bronze railing engraved with one thousand names of alumni donors. The planting design and installation was realized in collaboration with the respected horticulturalist Paul Ehnes from Greenery Unlimited.

awards
*2004 Award for Regional Citation, Canadian Society
of Landscape Architects (CSLA)*

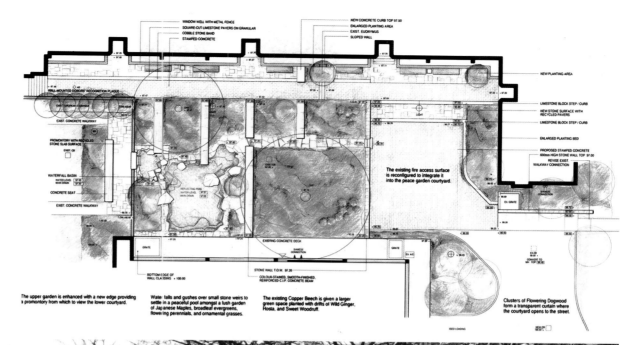

→ Illustrated concept plan.

↓ View from main entry of Garden in boulders in pool in winter.

↓↓ Urban plaza and splash pad.

The upper garden is enhanced with a new edge providing a promontory from which to view the lower courtyard.

Water falls and gushes over small stone weirs to settle in a peaceful pool amongst a lush garden of Japanese Maples, broadleaf evergreens, flowering perennials, and ornamental grasses.

The existing Copper Beech is given a larger green space planted with drifts of Wild Ginger, Hosta, and Sweet Woodruff.

Clusters of Flowering Dogwood form a transparent curtain where the courtyard opens to the street.

↑   View from upper terrace down to Garden.

←   Concrete slab piercing groundcover planting.

→   Sweet woodruff groundcover planting adjacent to stone pavers.

→→   Reflecting pool, boulder and concrete slabs at foot of majestic beech tree.

↑↑ Summer view of reflecting pool and waterfall.

← View from adjacent library.

↑ Illustrated perspective of waterfall and pool.

↗ Summer view of reflecting pool and waterfall.

→ Autumn view of reflecting pool and waterfall.

← The gentle sound of bubbling water soothes patients and visitors in the various sitting areas.

↓ Detail of water lily pool.

client
Withheld
other key consultants
Vermeulen / Hind Architects
location
Kitchener, Ontario
completion
2004
photography
Mary Jane Lovering

CNIB Headquarters Building

Vertechs Design Inc.

The Canadian National Institute for the Blind (CNIB) Headquarters building is a four storey building that occupies the same site as the original building which opened in 1954. The new Headquarters is a complex facility designed to set new standards of accessibility internationally for people who are blind, visually impaired and deafblind. As the country's primary provider of vision loss support services, the CNIB Headquarters building and landscape is a significant destination.

Vertechs Design Inc. landscape architects was selected to create an enticing series of landscaped spaces. The resultant solution was based on the same ground breaking principles which were the basis for the building's design, including universal accessibility, sustainability and longevity. The CNIB's Accessibility Coordinator Lesley MacDonald played a key role throughout the design phase, working together with the team to develop an accessible landscape that responds to the special needs of persons with vision loss.

The universally accessible facility encounters many visitors of all levels of ability. The landscape was designed to be enjoyed by employees, clients and visitors to the Headquarters. In 1956 the Garden Club of Toronto realized Elsinor Burns' concept of a Fragrant Garden on the grounds of the CNIB. The original garden no longer exists. However, its purpose to integrate accessibility with landscape design perseveres. These same principals were the origin for the new landscape design for the grounds surrounding the Headquarters.

The site is located on a prominent hilltop at the intersection of Bayview Avenue and Kilgour Road in midtown Toronto. A unique design response was required for the special population who will be using the facility.

Knowledge of way-finding and cueing techniques were important tools in the formation of the landscape. An accessible smooth concrete walkway bounded by lush planting leads people securely to the main entrance of the CNIB Headquarters building from the nearby intersection. As visitors approach the building the walkway changes to tactile,

→ Raised planters allow for fragrant plants to be appreciated by those using wheelchairs and those walking without bending.

↓ A dark tactile stone walkway delineates the most direct route through the garden.

dark coloured paving stone which leads to the building's main entrance. A tactile walking surface indicator composed of raised domes delineates the edge between pedestrian and vehicular circulation routes adjacent to the main entrance.

Just past the main entrance is the opening into the Fragrant Garden. The area is demarcated by a sign with large print and Braille. The most direct walking route through the Fragrant Garden is along the building wall, defined by dark, tactile paving stone. The main route is configured at right angles and straight lines to organize the space for those using a white cane.

Limestone screenings have been used to texturally distinguish the sitting nook areas within the garden from the circulation routes. The sound of the limestone under foot cues those with diminished vision to the fact that they have located a sitting area. The tactile surface is also accessible to those in wheelchairs. Dark flagstone bands separate the limestone from the concrete paving directing those using a white cane to sitting spots.

Curvilinear planter walls at waist height define sitting nooks throughout the garden. The raised planters allow for fragrant plants to be appreciated by those using wheelchairs and those walking by without bending. The sensory experience of the garden is heightened by fragrance, plant texture and a tactile ground plane.

A large pergola structure provides refuge from the sun on hot summer days. Fragrant flowering shrubs and perennials planted here challenge the senses. Plant material was chosen for its seasonal interest.

A designated enclosed guide dog relief area to the north of the Fragrant Garden includes a small guide dog run and water fountain for guide dogs.

The garden has met with success for all visitors through the provision of a secure, accessible and aesthetically pleasing environment.

↑ The large pergola structure provides relief from the sun and helps enclose several sitting nooks.

↘ Different wall heights and a variety of fragrant plants add visual interest and create depth within the Fragrant Garden.

↓ A bubbling water feature provides auditory interest and enhances the garden user's sensory experience.

↑　Concrete paving allows for universal accessibility.

↘　Trees, shrubs and perennials will grow to screen the parking lot from the main intersection nearby.

↓　Curvilinear planter walls delineate sitting areas throughout the garden.

client
Canadian National Institute for the Blind

other key consultants
Shore Tilbe Irwin Partners and Sterling Finlayson
  Architects in Joint Venture
Read Jones Christoffersen Ltd. Structural
  Engineers
Aecon Buildings

location
Toronto, Ontario

completion
2005

photography
Mary Jane Lovering, Viive Kittask

Corporate and Commercial

30 Adelaide Street East, Toronto

Janet Rosenberg + Associates Landscape Architects Inc.

We were initially approached by our client to develop a design identity for the landscape of this existing, international-style office building in the heart of downtown Toronto. Our vision for the site was to create a user-friendly space that was easily recognizable and visible from the street and a space that would become a landmark in downtown Toronto.

The landscape includes a central courtyard, an outdoor gathering area and several secondary landscape spaces created by the relationship of the building to its site. The central courtyard is dominated by two original majestic Ginkgo trees that were preserved during construction and contains a granite-surfaced arc flanked by stainless steel walls that direct visitors to the main entrance of the building. Sawn limestone cubes, scattered along the edge of the water feature, offer a place to sit and observe the activities of the surrounding urban environment and custom-designed site furnishings and planters add a finishing touch to this unique space.

Since its completion, this site has become a well-recognized space in the heart of downtown Toronto. By introducing new materials such as stainless steel as dominant elements of the landscape, the strong statement created by the distinct identity of this space challenges the public's perception of landscape design and the profession of landscape architecture.

The design identity established for this site represents a departure from the design and geometry of the building. It establishes the landscape as a separate element from the building, allowing us to use the landscape as an artistic and sculptural medium as a means of creating a distinct identity for the site. This site demonstrates a successful integration between art and the landscape in an effort to design a functional and user-friendly space in the heart of Toronto with a distinct identity.

↗ Aerial view of courtyard and casual seating.

→ Aerial view of court which incorporates a bold sweeping granite arc, flanked by elegant stainless steel walls and balanced on either side by two stately Gingko trees.

← The composition of elements creates a playful atmosphere, successfully integrating art and landscape in the heart of Toronto.

↓ Casual cube clusters create seating at pool edge.

↓↓ Fountain detail.

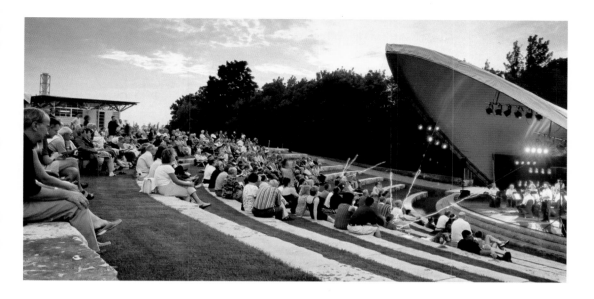

↖ Patrons of the winery enjoy entertainment at the custom Amphitheatre that was carved out of the landscape.

↓ Bench detail.

↙ A garden of green and burgundy foliage; representing wines created at the winery.

← Bench as example of custom detailing.

client
Vincor International
other key consultants
Aldershot Landscape Contractors Ltd.
Source Design
Merit Contractors Niagara
Kuwabara Payne McKenna Blumberg Architects
location
Niagara-on-the-Lake , Ontario
completion
September 2001
photography
Neil Fox

Taboo

Janet Rosenberg + Associates Landscape Architects Inc.

The design vision for the entrance feature, temporary parking lot and clubhouse facility at this golf course in the Muskoka region was to use the site as a medium for transforming nature into art, and in doing so, inspire a new appreciation and understanding of this natural environment. We chose to use rustic materials that would react over time to natural processes in an effort to express the dynamic and reversible nature of the regional environment.

We used this vision to create a distinct identity for the site, an identity that has been adopted for the entire golf course and future resort development. The principal components of this project include angular entrance feature walls made of locally quarried granite; a thirty foot tall sculptural tree made of corten steel; a gravel parking lot and granite river stone parking lot islands with compositions of granite boulders and weathered, upright logs; sandblasted concrete cubes that define the parking spaces; light standards wrapped with wire mesh trellises covered in vines; the clubhouse, a dramatic composition made of perforated, backlit corten steel and clusters of sawn logs, and a sculpted front lawn in front of the clubhouse.

Large masses of predominantly indigenous plant material in combinations of texture, form and colour are distributed throughout the site, including a pond that provides a scenic setting for the clubhouse. The banks of the pond were planted with marginal plant species in an effort to re-vegetate and stabilize the slopes, as well as contend with fluctuating water levels caused by the golf course irrigation system. In an effort to achieve a successful integration with the surrounding context, numerous large specimens of both coniferous and deciduous trees were brought in and planted throughout the site.

awards
2004 Merit Award, National Post Design Exchange
  Awards;
2003 Regional Merit Award, Design Category,
  Canadian Society of Landscape Architects.

↖ Clubhouse wall detail inspired by the beauty and character of the surrounding natural landscape.
↑ Sandblasted tree trunks as sculptural elements in the parking area.
→ Entrance sculpture.
↓ Planting composition.
← Staircase to main clubhouse entrance.

client
Muskoka Sands Resort
other key consultants
Great Gulf Group
Oriole Landscaping Ltd
Prototype Design Lab
Versus Design
location
Gravenhurst, Ontario
completion
September 2002
photography
Neil Fox

Kicking Horse Mountain Resort

Tom Barratt Ltd

Kicking Horse Mountain Resort is the first new four-season resort to open in the Canadian Rockies in 25 years. The area is the exalted meeting place of the Rockies, the Purcells and the Selkirks, three of the continent's most majestic ranges and six National Parks surround the Resort – Banff, Glacier, Kootenay, Yoho, Mt. Revelstoke and Jasper.

The proposed mountain village and master planned community includes 3,000 bed units - a mix of townhouses, single family residences, condominium lodges, hotels and B&Bs as well as a multitude of shops, bars, restaurants and other commercial amenities that suit a four-season alpine resort.

'Kicking Horse Mountain Resort' is named after the renowned river and the high-alpine pass that were key to the opening of the Canadian West, and as such, the name evokes a sense of discovery, exploration and history.'

The village and plaza draws upon the rugged nature of the Rockies and utilizes natural features including water, rock outcroppings, large boulders and natural planting.

The village and plaza is to be unique in ski resorts and it is to draw upon the past and the rugged nature of the local rockies around. Historical reference, local materials is the basis for developing guidelines & design.

Tom Barratt Ltd. is working on overall planning and detailed village & plaza design.

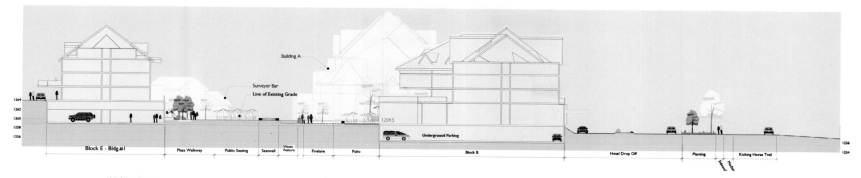

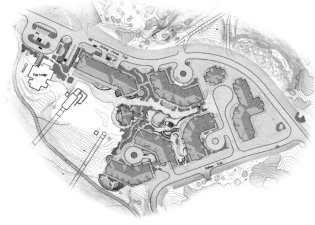

↑ ↑ Site Section of Plaza.
↑ Rendering of Plaza Plan Concept.
↗ Rocky Mountains.
↓ 3D Terrain & Buildings View.

↑ Plaza Landscaping.
← Landscape plan of Summit.
↓ Sections of Summit.

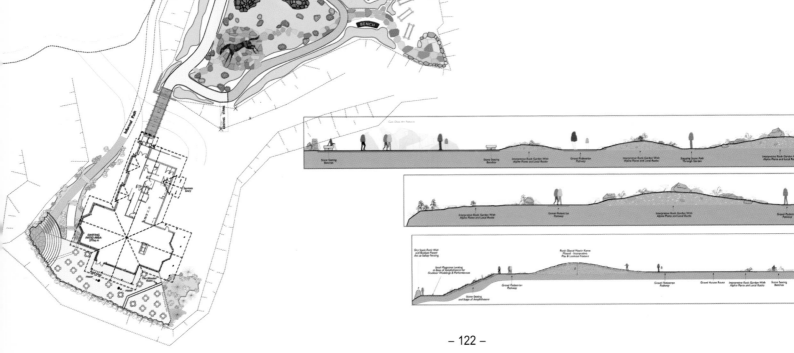

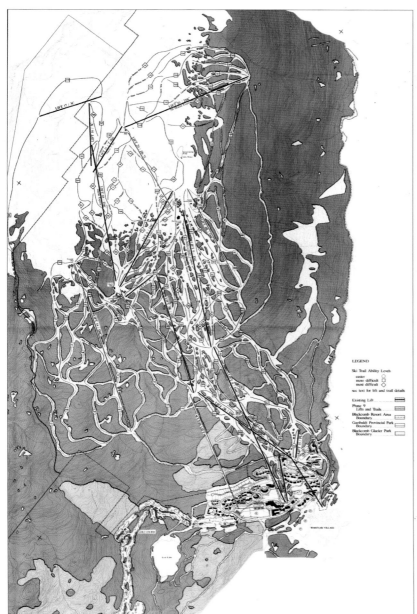

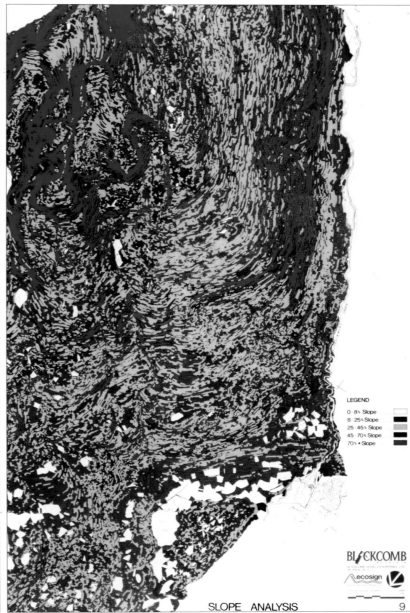

SLOPE ANALYSIS

LEGEND

0 - 8% Slope
8 - 25% Slope
25 - 45% Slope
45 - 70% Slope
70% + Slope

BLACKCOMB

ecosign

9

↑   Blackcomb master plan.
↗   Blackcomb Mountain slope analysis.
→   Blackcomb 3D model.

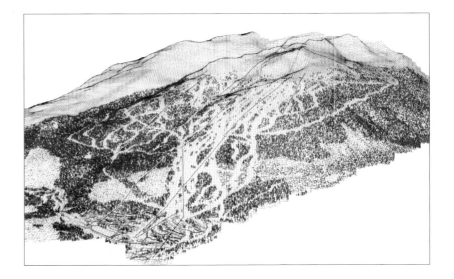

↑ Aerial view of Whistler Blackcomb
Resort.

↗ The Whistler village.

→ Whistler Mountain master plan.

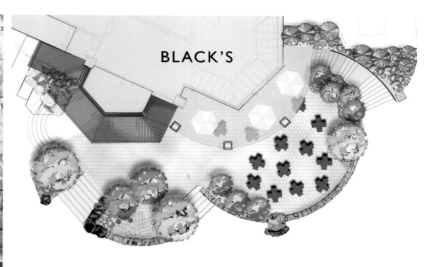

BLACK'S

← Art Piece on Site.
↑ Rendered Illustration of the Landscape Plan.
↘ Fun Exploring Blacks Art / Water Feature.
↓ Blacks Patio.

client
Black's Ristorante
other key consultants
Artist: Robert Studer
location
Whistler, BC
completion
November, 2003
photography
Tom Barratt

Parks, Gardens and Memorial

Toronto Botanical Garden
PMA Landscape Architects Ltd.

awards
2007 Canadian Society of Landscape Architects
  (CSLA) Award for Regional Citation
2007 Society for Environmental Design (SEGD)
  Award – Signage & Wayfinding
2006 Landscape Ontario Water Conservation Award
2006 Design Exchange Gold Award for Landscape
  Architecture
2006 City of Toronto - Green Toronto Award for
  Design
2006 Leadership in Energy and Environmental Design
  (LEED) Silver Certification

The revitalized Toronto Botanical Garden opened ceremoniously in September 2006. This project is the first stage towards a larger vision to develop a botanical garden of international stature: a horticultural collection displayed in uniquely designed spaces. Designers PMA Landscape Architects Ltd. and Thomas Sparling Inc. led the landscape consultant team, in collaboration with renowned horticulturist Paul Ehnes. Collectively, the consultant team had to respond to the goal of attracting a broader range of the general public through innovative design and programming.

By providing unique environments in which to profile a wide diversity of plant material, the planting and their environs have become inspiring and educational. The park development includes a variety of garden types, feature earthworks, custom walls and structures, and special paving. The twelve new contemporary gardens include a Knot Garden, Terrace Garden, Herb & Kitchen Garden, Show Garden, Spiral Mound, Carpet Bed Garden, Teaching Garden, Floral Hall Courtyard, Garden Hall Courtyard, West View Terrace, Nature's Garden and Water Garden. The concept of displaying botanical collections in contemporary garden spaces is unique to TBG, and Canada as a whole.

In addition to its horticultural and educational objectives, TBG wanted to promote its identity as a wholly inclusive facility. An overriding principle was to ensure the site and building design welcomes physically challenged visitors as well as those from multicultural communities typical of Toronto. It was PMA who expanded the mandate to include a sustainable design objective. Some of the sustainable elements include an extensive green roof on the building, rainwater collection and infiltration systems, and the reuse of salvaged materials as features of new elements such as the recycled bottles and bricks in the custom Terrace Garden wall. The building addition was similarly designed to achieve a Leadership in Energy and Environmental Design (LEED) Silver Certification.

→ Illustrated concept plan.
↓ View from Arrival Courtyard towards new building addition.

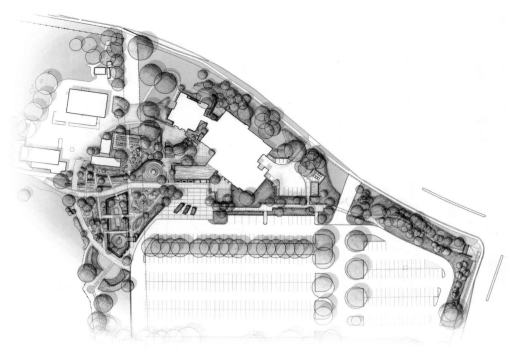

Aerial view of Arrival Courtyard.

©Tom Arban

↑   View to Building with Terrace Garden
     in foreground.

↗   Building addition with adjacent Knot
     Garden.

→   View of gardens with newly-planted
     Knot Garden in foreground.

←   Spiral Mound with Herb & Kitchen
     Garden metal planters in foreground.

↑↑ Spiral Mound in winter.

↑   Elevation of the feature earthwork,
     Spiral Mound.

↗   Visitors ascending the Spiral Mound.

→   Detail of salvaged cobblestones to
     create Spiral Mound walkway.

©Tom Arban

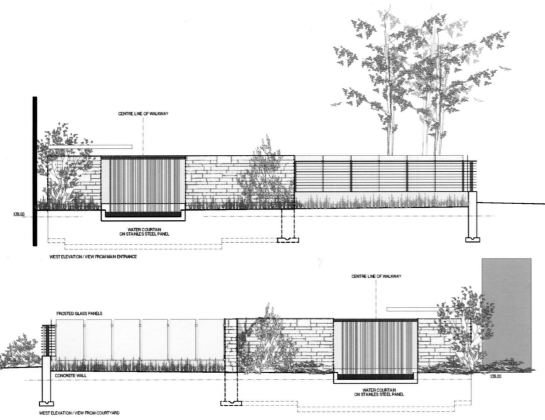

CENTRE LINE OF WALKWAY

WATER COURTAIN
ON STAINLES STEEL PANEL

139.00

WEST ELEVATION / VIEW FROM MAIN ENTRANCE

CENTRE LINE OF WALKWAY

FROSTED GLASS PANELS

CONCRETE WALL

139.00

WATER COURTAIN
ON STAINLES STEEL PANEL

WEST ELEVATION / VIEW FROM COURTYARD

↑ Floral Hall courtyard walls and reed
planting.

← Elevation of the Floral Hall Courtyard
walls and water feature.

↑   Floral Hall courtyard with existing building.

↘↘ Custom metal gate at Floral Hall courtyard.

↘   Custom chain-mail water feature at building entrance.

↓   Floral Hall courtyard walls and reed planting.

↑ Stone bridge and water canal between Westview Terrace and Garden Hall Courtyard.
↗ Metal planter walls and planting at Terrace Garden.
→ Metal planter walls and planting at Terrace Garden.
↘ Aerial view of Westview Terrace and gardens in background.
↓ Canal and courtyard at Westview Terrace.

↑ Detail winter view of earthwork wall
   containing salvaged bottles and stone.

↗ Detail of terminus of Terrace Garden
   earthwork structure.

↗↗ Reinforced earthwork structure
   containing salvaged materials .

→→ Metal planter walls and planting at
   Terrace Garden.

→ Winter view of Terrace Garden.

↖↖ Herb and Kitchen Garden with Show Garden in background.

↖ Wood fence backdrop to Herb and Kitchen Garden.

↑ Trellis and climbing plants at Herb and Kitchen Garden entrance.

↗ Custom wayfinding signage panels.

←← Metal planters and plant-stands in Herb and Kitchen Garden.

← Metal planters and plant-stands in Herb and Kitchen Garden.

client
Toronto Botanical Garden
location
Toronto, Ontario
other key consultants
Landscape Architect collaborator: Thomas
  Sparling inc.
Planting Designer: Paul Ehnes, Greenery Unlimited
Horticulturist: Cathie Cox, Toronto Botanical
  Garden
Entry Garden Designer: Martin Wade Landscape
  Architects with Piet Oudolf
Building Architect: Montgomery Sisam Architects
Signage & Wayfinding Designer: A+a – Adams +
  Associates Design Consultants
Mechanical Engineer: EMC Group Limited
Electrical Engineer: Rybka, Smith & Ginsler Ltd.
Structural Engineer: Blackwell Engineering Ltd.
completion
Fall 2006
photography
PMA Landscape Architects Ltd. unless stated

Barrel Warehouse Park

Janet Rosenberg + Associates Landscape Architects Inc.

Barrel Warehouse Park was conceived as a city park for the new downtown core of Uptown Waterloo. It is located in the area of the historic Seagram distilleries, adjacent to two former barrel warehouses converted into condominiums.

Our design intent was to create a public park that reflected the industrial heritage of the site as well as the contemporary characteristics of the high-tech industry that is predominant in Waterloo. Consequently, we chose to use a combination of traditional and contemporary materials, most with industrial qualities, and we used several salvaged industrial artifacts as sculptural pieces throughout the site. We incorporated a large area of ornamental grasses, suggesting the grains used in the distilling process, which is bisected by elevated, industrial catwalks. The park also includes sculpted lawn areas; concrete planters with sculpted hedges, traditional rubble-stone walls and a contemporary architectural cut-stone wall and water feature combination that connects two distinctly separate areas of the park.

The most predominant and visible features of Barrel Warehouse Park are the large-scale, industrial artifacts used as sculptural pieces throughout the site. We incorporated these artifacts as artistic installations that reflect the industrial heritage of the site.

From the beginning of the project, we strove to create the proper cultural conditions for the plant material used in the park in order to ensure their long-term survival and success. The entire site was sub-soiled prior to construction and five different soil mixes were used in the planting areas throughout the site. We designed large, connected planters for the street trees wherever possible and where space was limited, we used structural soil to extend the volume of soil available to the trees under the paving.

awards
2004 Silver Award, National Post Design Exchange Awards;
2003 Regional Merit Award, Design Category, Canadian Society of Landscape Architects.

→ View across linear planting scheme to façade of historic building.

↓ Overall view of the park's clean geometry.

↖↖ Custom benches interlaced with undulating sculpted lawn.

↖ Water feature at small court area.

← Trees planted in bands along the streetscape utilize a structural soil planting method.

→ Composition and pallet of materials.

↓ Court as foreground for condominium development.

Over-scaled industrial artifacts
serve as sculptural elements.

← The center axis of the central fountain, with 10 foot waterfalls.

↑ Custom designed 'Adirondak' chairs.

↗ Beacon plinths march up the grass slope.

client
Concord Pacific Group Inc.

other key consultants
R.M. Erickson Landscape Architecture,
Cochrane Engineering,
Thurber Engineering,
Holland Landscapers,
Vincent Helton & Associates

location
Vancouver, British Columbia

completion
2004

photography
Alex Piro

Harbour Green II
PWL Partnership Landscape Architects Inc

Harbour Green II is a distinct neighbourhood park, situated at the heart of the Coal Harbour development in downtown Vancouver. The design responds to a master plan that addressed the reuse of land occupied by the Canadian Pacific Railway for over a century along the downtown waterfront. This park is significant as a public space that reclaims this area, as well as greening the city, and contributing to the continuity of green space and urban wildlife corridors that connect the city dweller to the waterfront seawall/bikeway systems.

Harbour Green II is the central open space in the new Coal Harbour neighbourhood. It features a children's spray pool and park restaurant, a decorative escarpment wall, intricate paving patterns, and art deco details. The urban character, and a location near Stanley Park and the cruise ship docks called for a distinct design. This has resulted in an aesthetic that embraces the old world urban park style, in addition to features that tell the story of the pre-industrial history of the site by illustrating the old shoreline, including grass covered earth waves that reference the texture of the ocean.

Despite the complex design of this park and the high level of detail, the construction budget was a consideration. Therefore common materials have been utilized in the design. These include pre-cast concrete, as well as standard light fixtures with custom elements that respond to the art deco design theme. The water-play area doubles as a decorative fountain when the weather is cool and includes a filtering and recirculation system as an environmentally responsible approach to the challenge of providing a large water park. PWL Partnership's role on Harbour Green II began with the rezoning of the land and ended with the completion of the detailed design, a process that took fifteen years to complete.

↑ Planting at the easterly end of Harbour Green II.
↓ Open lawn, water feature and floating walkway with Coal Harbour and the North Shore Mountains as its backdrop.

↖ Period benches under shade trees mark the urban edge of the walkway/bikeway.

↑ The water feature.

→ The water feature doubles as a children's spray pool.

← Winding pathway making it's way to one of four minor promontory lookouts.

client
Vancouver Board of Parks and Recreation,
Fairmont Development Ltd.
other key consultants
Sandwell Engineering Inc.;
Darwin Construction (Western) Ltd.;
Wilco Landscape Contractors Ltd.
location
Vancouver, British Columbia
completion
2002
photography
Alex Piro

Place St-Roch

WAA

Saint-Roch Garden was designed as the key element of an urban renewal project, aimed at rehabilitating the old lower city neighbourhood of St-Roch, in Québec City. The park was created as the first step in the revitalisation of the area, to encourage developers to take advantage of the available sites for construction and thus proceed with the rehabilitation of the entire area. The city's objective was to create confidence in this area, to bring new development, improve the environment, and the economical situation of the whole neighbourhood.

The design of the Garden takes its roots in the local history of the city, and its natural environment. Using an "analogy" to the natural environment of the city of Quebec, the design is modern and bold. Using the 10-meter natural grade difference on the site, the garden is divided in 2 specific areas. The top portion represents the Capt Diamant with its natural features. The lower portion is designed as an urban garden. The main feature of the garden, the cascade, represents a famous waterfall in the area. The stone details of the fountain are inspired by the natural geology of the Capt Diamant, but treated in a modern and architectural way. The various water basins create different water characters, some narrow and rapid, others large and grandiose such as the final fall.

The vegetation in the escarpment is all-native and thus represents the natural vegetation on the escarpment. In the lower garden, more horticultural planting provides rich flowering tree shrubs and perennials.

The project was very successful, both in terms of planning, the entire neighbourhood was rehabilitated; as well as for the quality of the design and the ambiance of this rich green oasis.

awards
*1994 National Award, Canadian Society of
Landscape Architects.*

→ Modern signature lighting design specially for this garden.
↘ A night view of the main cascade.
↓ General view looking from the Upper City.

↑   General view towards the waterfall.
↗   View of the gazebo while entering the garden from the upper entrance.
↗↗ Partial view of the main water cascade.
↓   The lower reflecting pool and the cascade.

← The green carpet and the Gazebo, in the back the new in-fill architecture overlooking the garden.

↓ One of the annual planting borders.

↙ The green carpet, the waterfall in the back, and the escarpment planted with native plants.

client
City of Quebec
other key consultants
Option Aménagement
Morelli Design
Letellier Cyr architects
location
Quebec City, Quebec
completion
1993

Downsview Memorial Parkette - MOTH Gardens

Jeannie Thib, Artist
Scott Torrance Landscape Architect Inc.

The design of MOTH Gardens is inspired by Downsview's history of aviation. At the core of the gardens a limestone sculpture refers to the first airplanes manufactured in Downsview - the Gypsy and Tiger Moths. Built in the de Havilland factory, they were first flown by civilians out of local flying clubs and later by World War II pilots. The artwork was inspired by a photograph from the 1920s showing the word MOTH written in large white letters on the turf beside the original Downsview airstrip. The sculpture's stone sections of varying heights, which also serve as tables and seating, coalesce into the letters MOTH when seen from above.

A vine covered steel arbour at the west side of the gardens incorporates various aircraft references including tear drop shaped sections modeled on the interior structure of a wing. A row of windsocks marks the park's eastern end. The central grassy "airstrip" is defined by a line of blue solar runway lights and plantings of tall maiden grasses. Blue LED light strips attached under the stones cast a soft blue outline around the MOTH letters at night.

Each letter of the MOTH sculpture is surrounded by a unique garden. These rose, flowering annual, scented herb and butterfly gardens are intersected by walkways patterned on Italian Renaissance garden designs in recognition of the area's early Italian immigrants. On either side of the gardens groups of blossoming pear trees refer to the many orchards that once dotted the area. A grove of lilacs on the north side of the "airstrip" also pays tribute to the agricultural and settlement history of the Keele and Wilson neighbourhood.

Downsview Memorial Parkette was originally dedicated in 1946 to honour local people who sacrificed their lives in World War II. A dedication to them is inscribed in the low stone wall that makes up one section of the O. MOTH Gardens serves as a meaningful community landmark and provides a green oasis in the midst of a very busy urban environment. The moth, symbolically associated with spirit, serves as a touchstone for both the memorial nature of the parkette's origins and for a vibrant and continually changing community.

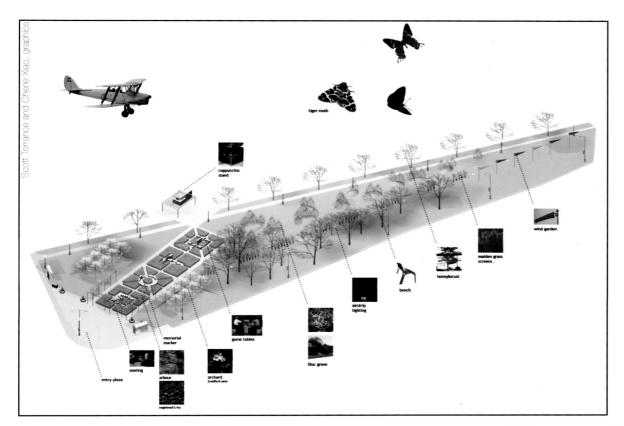

tiger moth

cappuccino stand

wind garden

maiden grass screens

honeylocust

bench

airstrip lighting

game tables

lilac grove

memorial marker

seating

arbour

orchard bradford pear

entry plaza

engelman's ivy

↑ Memorial dedication in the O garden.
↗ The butterfly garden around the H.
↓ The rose garden and chess board.

↖ The Arbour.
↑ Windsocks at the 'airstrip'.
↙ Flower, scented and butterfly gardens.
← The Plaza.

client
The City of Toronto
location
Toronto
other key consultants
Lighting design: Lightstudio Inc.;
Electrical engineers: Smith and Andersen electrical
 engineers;
Structural engineers: Peter Sheffield & Associates
 Ltd.;
graphics: Cherie Xiao.
completion
June 2006
photography
Jose San Juan (Copyright Jose San Juan, City of
 Toronto). Scott Torrance and Josh Randell

The First Nations Garden, Montreal

The First Nations Garden was built to commemorate the peace treaty signed 300 years ago between the eleven Quebec First Nations and the government of La Nouvelle-France. Although it covers only 2 hectares in the heart of the Montreal Botanical Gardens, its significance is great.

The design concept celebrates the profound relationship of native people with the land and their considerable contribution to the development of Canada. Often called a "healing garden", the concept of the FNG serves the needs of native people and promotes understanding between people of all origins. The landscape design of the garden expresses the common ground shared by the eleven nations in a most powerful and evocative manner. The contemporary treatment of structures and details reflects the forward-looking vision of these thriving nations, as they meet new challenges in our society. An interpretation strategy was developed, based on their history, myths, crafts and extensive knowledge of plants. The garden displays cultural and scientific aspects that can be appreciated at different levels. Visitors are encouraged to rediscover their roots and place within natural cycles.

The FNG was developed with the support and input of the eleven nations. A native staff person conveyed authentic information. The garden is accessible by 3 entrances or "doors". The design is inspired by traces left after the native tents are removed. These circular patterns are also "universal" shapes used for many native artefacts and works of art. With inscriptions in Native, French and English languages, the doors are a welcoming and an integration space. After entering the garden, visitors discover a world of plants and culture. The space is divided in 2 ecosystems, the forest of the north, mainly evergreen, and the deciduous forest of the south. The creation of an authentic understory planting reveals not only the native trees, but also a real and complex forest environment celebrating native plants. Thematic areas such as the "agricultural farmers of the south", the summer and winter camps, and the water environment illustrates various aspects of these proud and creative cultures.

↑   The Totem is a native way of expressing
different relationships with nature, the cycles,
and the life.

← In this area, the northern environment was represented by large stone surfaces, aquatic plants, and native trees.

↓ The northern people live in a difficult environment, they use stone signals such as this original "innunkshuck" to provide direction, food, and clothing to travelers.

↙ The summer campground is in direct relationship to the waterways; here a circular path allows visitors to see medicinal and aquatic plants.

← The pavilion is modern and perfectly integrated in the landscape.

↙ Inspired by the agriculture nations this structure is similar to the "long houses" where several families lived in community.

↙↙ The winter campground in the middle of the woods (called "le terrier de l'ours!")

→ A portable summer structure commonly used by most nations.

client
City of Montreal Botanical Garden of Montreal
other key consultants
Saucier Perrotte et Associés
Cultura Inc
DES design inc.
location
Montréal, Québec
completion
2002

Riverwood
du Toit Allsopp Hillier
du Toit Architects

Mississauga is a growing city of 500,000 on the outskirts of Toronto. Created three decades ago by the amalgamation of a number of villages, the new suburban city has an emerging urban core which now includes Riverwood. The 150 Acre garden park and natural preserve is a former rural estate, rich in the Arts and Crafts style, overlooking the banks of the Credit River at the geographic centre of the City.

The site had once been harvested for lumber and worked in part for farming. Ironically, after many years of second generation growth, Riverwood now remains one of the more environmentally significant landscapes in Mississauga, although until recently few people knew it existed.

The culmination of years of careful planning by the City of Mississauga, the first phase of an overall master plan has recently been realized and the transformation of the land into a public garden park has begun. The components of this phase included the renovation of existing heritage buildings, a new facility for an art school, an extensive network of trails, parking areas, storm water management systems, revitalization of existing wetlands and an approach to the landscaping that features the heritage and environmental qualities of the site.

Protecting the parks cultural integrity was a key challenge. The general composition of the park responds to the historic property grid and former agricultural terraces, overlaid on the dramatic topography of the site. The new entry drive builds on the winding arrival sequence of the former estate

awards
2006 Award of Merit for Architecture, City of
  Mississauga Urban Design Awards;
2006 People's Choice Award, City of Mississauga
  Urban Design Awards.

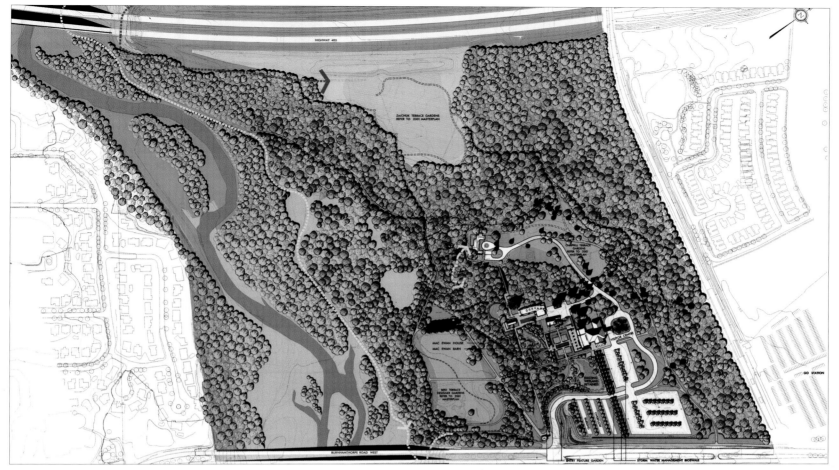

↑   The master plan of Riverwood.

drive, consisting of broad swaths of naturalized plant material hugging the rising sweep of the drive just inside the entry. An alleé of deciduous trees are planted along the parking lot edges to shade a walkway as well as to recall the former farm lanes and orchards of the site.

The complex hydrological functions and ecological habitats of the site are maintained and enhanced through storm water buffers with passive drainage and water management initiatives such as bioswales incorporated into the parking lot and roadway designs. In this way water quality and flow are controlled as it passes through sensitive wetlands, MacEwan Creek, and the Credit River floodplain.

The design strategy for the new building and site elements drew from the arts and crafts heritage and vernacular traditions of the existing buildings, but in a contemporary way, with the understanding that these structures will set the standard for any future development in the park. A clear, respectful distinction between old and new is established by extracting from the palate of materials and construction techniques of the existing and applying current thinking to the new.

The MacEwan House, a modest farmhouse, built in mid to late 19th century was renovate to accommodate a broad range of new program elements while maintaining the historical character. The direction for the design was to retain and reinforce elements that had heritage significance while updating the services and structure of the building to today's standards.

One of the more significant heritage structures on the site, the MacEwan Barn, is believed to be one of the oldest barn structures still remaining within the City of Mississauga. The structure exhibits traditional material and construction techniques of the pre-industrial age and despite its condition, the heritage value warranted an initiative to make it a feature within the park, converting it into an interpretive centre.

The siting of the first new building on the site responses to the adjacent heritage buildings and reinforces the overall composition of the MacEwan terrace. This new facility provides teaching facilities and display spaces for Visual Arts Mississauga (VAM). A simple, understated building containing five flexible studios, display gallery, administrative support spaces and a public comfort station for the park. It was important that VAM be sited so that the relationship between the House and the Barn was maintained and that the overall composition would create a common outdoor space. Through a desire to connect artists with nature and the public with art, the building developed from a series of solid walls arranged in a landscape, separated by glazing, allowing a high level of transparency. A number of 'green' initiatives have also been incorporated into the building, including a future green roof, strong horizontal shading projections and the use of clerestorey and north facing windows to provide extensive natural day lighting and ventilation.

Riverwood represents the first step in the realization of what will inevitably be one of Mississauga's principal cultural and environmental assets and will serve as a precedent for similar sites in the future.

↑ Spruce Alley, the original orchard wind break.

↗ The original Riverwood Arts & Crafts residence Chappell Estate cira 1920.

↗↗ A Mixture of hard and soft landscaping helps nestle the existing MacEwan House into the setting.

→ The oldest structure on the site, the MacEwan Barn is thought to be built around 1860.

↓ John Hillier's hand render depicts the character of the site, while showing the relationship of the components of the park.

East-West Cross Section

North-South Cross Section

→   Visual Arts Mississauga (VAM) at dusk.
↓   VAM entry: wood and steel canopy provides shelter. Natural stone is used for building cladding and landscape walks.
↘   MacEwan House and VAM nestled into landscape. Engineered retaining wall holds back land, allowing access to basement of house.

→ Early concept rendering of VAM, MacEwan Barn and potential gardens.

↘ Composition of three: VAM near completion on left, MacEwan Barn in background, MacEwan House on right and white pines beyond.

↘↘ Early concept rendering of VAM (left), MacEwan Barn in background, MacEwan House (right) with terreced landscape.

↑   Newly constructed parking lot biaswale.

↗   Limestone swale inlet.

↓   Stormwater detention wetland.

↑ MacEwan House garden terrace.
↗ Visual Arts Studio building.
↓ Valley boardwalk on nature trail.

client
City of Mississauga
other key consultants
Architects: du Toit Architects Limited;
Environmental Landscape Architect: ENVision
   – The Hough Group;
Architectural Heritage: Nicholas Holman;
Landscape Heritage: Pleasance Crawford;
Civil Engineer: McCormick Rankin Corporation;
Structural Engineer: Ian Dunlop & Associates
   Limited;
Mechanical Engineer: Tou & Associates Ltd.;
Electrical Engineer: McDonnell Engineering Inc.;
General Contractor: Gateman-Milloy Inc..
location
Mississauga, Ontario
completion
2005
photography
du Toit Allsopp Hillier

Stanley Park Salmon Stream
PWL Partnership Landscape Architects Inc

Stanley Park provides the City of Vancouver with 1000 acres of forest and waterfront land in the center of the city. At the same time, the salmon is a key economic and cultural figure in British Columbia.

The Stanley Park Salmon Stream is an interactive display and educational feature that introduces park visitors to the life cycle of the salmon first hand. The project also represents the dramatic transformation of an asphalt parking lot into a natural stream habitat. The upper portion of the stream, and the beach at the Seining Pool are completely accessible to park visitors, who stroll along the edge, and over a series of pedestrian bridges. The lower section of the stream is connected to the harbour, allowing salmon migrate to the ocean, and make their way up to the Seining Pool on their return. One of the key goals during the design process was to effectively capture stormwater in a re-circulating system, and to recharge the lower portion of the stream with saltwater from the Vancouver Aquarium's whale pools. This has been accomplished through the separation of the two systems with a weir, camouflaged as a logjam. The resulting design incorporates natural rocks, roots, weathered logs, and native shrubs and groundcover into the landscape, and features a new fish habitat that describes the salmon's life cycle and the challenges associated with mitigating environmental damage over time.

In 1998, 14,000 fry were released into the ocean along with an organic molecule producing a scent to help adult fish find their way back, and since 2001, the salmon have returns to the site each year. The fact that Pink, Chum and Coho Salmon have returned to spawn is a testament to its great success of this project as fish habitat, and an outdoor educational exhibit.

Pedestrian bridge that connects the salmon stream with the Vancouver Aquarium.

← A man made weir that separates the salt water and fresh water portions of the stream.

↑ The stream below the homing pond.

↗ Planting along the stream.

→ Small gravel beach constructed with a combination of sculpted gunite concrete and river rock.

client
Vancouver Board of Parks and Recreation
other key consultants
Pottinger Gaherty Environmental Consultants;
Earth Tech Canada Consulting Engineers;
Matcon Civil Constructors Inc.;
Moscone Brothers Landscaping Ltd.
location
Vancouver, British Columbia
completion
1999
photography
Alex Piro

Beach Park

WAA

Located on the former Expo 67 site, and a few minutes from downtown Montreal, this 65 acre recreational park provides a unique and naturalistic approach to creating an "urban beach". Easily accessible by subway, bus, car, and bicycle, this unique public park is cherished by the citizens.

In a completely man made environment, the park and the surrounding gardens offer a very natural and ecological feeling. Using the natural water from the St-Laurence River, three wetland ponds were built in a naturalistic design and planted with more than 100,000 native aquatic plants. The water from the beach is directed in the wetland where it is filtered and then returned to the beach after being treated with UV lights. Inspired by the natural geology of the northern lakes of Quebec, the winding sand strip, grass and plantation provide a natural and pleasing feeling. Designed to accommodate up to 6,000 visitors a day, the beach is open daily during the summer.

In addition to the beach area, a sailing school provides classes as well as boat rental for people visiting the island park. Construction details are simple and rustic; stone, wood and metal are the chosen materials for buildings as well as landscape elements such as benches lights, drinking fountain etc. A continuous concrete walk way offers easy and convenient circulation for pedestrians and for maintenance. The Chalet pavilion containing a restaurant, boutiques, changing rooms, shower rooms, lockers, and toilets is fully integrated into the landscape. This provides a large and open, but protected terrace overlooking the beach, the sailing school, and in the distance, the Casino. This project has received many awards for its design and unique ecological aspects such as the reconstructed wetland and purification system.

awards
National Honor, Canadian Society of Landscape Architects.

↑   A General view of the sandy beach from the Sailing School.

↓   The filtered water from the wetlands exits into the beach area as a natural spring.

↑ Reconstructed wetlands were built to filter the water from the beach area. Largely inspired by local
↗ ecosystems, 3 ponds with more than 100,000 plants were constructed as an alternative ecological filtering system.

↗↗ The sandy beach was designed as a "Laurentian" resort. In the distance, you can see the Sailing School and the Montreal Casino.

→ The Sailing School, with boat rental and fishing docks.

↘ Early morning view of the beach and lake.

↓ One of the wetland's ponds with educational panels. In the back, there is a partial view of downtown Montreal.

↖ A few minutes from downtown Montreal, this is the biggest sailing school in the Province of Quebec.

↑ The rental area and in the back, an area specially designed and restricted to swimming.

← Formal classes and public boat rental are available throughout the summer.

client
City of Montreal
location
Montréal, Québec
completion
1990

Safe Zone

Stoss Landscape Urbanism

Stoss conceived and oversaw the installation of "Safe Zone," a reformulated pleasure garden utilizing a range of off-the-shelf safety products turned or stretched to new ends. The garden was recently installed at the 7th International Gardens Festival at Jardins de Metis / Reford Gardens in Grand-Metis, Quebec. The garden utilizes an array of commercial products designed for potentially dangerous conditions and situations, yet turned to playful uses: poured-in-place rubber surfacing, plastic warning strips, traction mats, goal post bumpers—materials of everyday landscapes (subway platforms, sidewalks, playgrounds, sports fields) isolated and coerced into a provocative and interactive garden installation.

The garden's main feature is a poured-in-place rubber surfacing, typically only installed in playground environments to cushion falls. Yet the material is amazingly tactile—soft, squishy, destabilizing. We imagined that it could be manipulated and exploited three-dimensionally so as to create an exterior rubber room—protective, comforting, yet somehow physically alienating, somewhat akin to climbing aboard a small, tippy boat, or jumping on a mattress. Intriguingly, what is often stripped away by codes and regulations—uncertainty, danger of falling—is retained and amplified via rubber's inherent physical, material qualities.

The realized garden is a topography of code and regulation—essentially manufactured, three-dimensional garden conditions (hillocks and valleys) that require protective measures and materials according to playground codes and regulations. The garden's undulating, synthetic surface was stretched (literally poured) over a rippling, activated groundplane woven into a clearing in the

↑ Overview of safe zone.

↘ Section.

woods. The rubber surface was supplemented by pools of loose rubber granules into which one could burrow or bounce; one pool was unbounded, at the seam between rubber and forest litter, and allowed to spread via foot traffic and activity—allowing the rubber to contaminate the woodland, creating a gradient of synthetic to organic materials. The result was tactile, playful, but insidious.

Safe Zone is the pleasure garden reformulated and updated, a contemporary reinterpretation of a classic garden type: playful; tactile; sensual; engaging; uncertain; perhaps even risky.

←   Overview of safe zone.
→   Plan.
↓   Children running up and down rubber hills.

© Louise Tanguey

↖ Workman relaxing on the rubber surface.

↑ Safe zone with tree bumpers and forest.

↘ Safe zone with forest in foreground.

↓ Edge condition of detectable warning strip and rubber hillock.

↙ Children running up and down rubber hills.

← Child running up and down rubber hills.

Courtesy of Stoss

Courtesy of Stoss

client/owner
International Garden Festival, Jardins de Métis /
Reford Gardens
location
Grand-Métis, Québec
design team at stoss
Chris Reed (Principal), Chris Muskopf, Scott Bishop,
Kristin Malone, Graham Palmer.
other key consultants
services + materials donated or discounted by Cape
Fear Systems,
Solplast, SofSurfaces, Jim Knowles + Paul
Wellington, Recovery
Technologies, U.S. Rubber Recycling and
SofSolutions
completion
June 2006

Rocky Point Park
van der Zalm + associates, Inc.

The Rocky Point Park Master Plan Revitalization Project was an opportunity to re-imagine the City of Port Moody's premier urban waterfront park into a multi-functional series of dynamic spaces that would communicate the rich history of the city and the area through its art integrated public and natural facilities.

In the summer of 2003, the City of Port Moody, British Columbia set out to re-vitalize its premier 9 hectare urban waterfront park within its downtown core. Although well used by the general community, Rocky Point Park was in need of a re-imagining of its current masterplan. It was hoped that this park could become the premier public gathering place for the community during its signature "Golden Spike Days" as well as become a contact point for the community to interact and experience the Burrard inlet shoreline and the last untouched mud flat ecosystem in the lower mainland. The primary purpose of this project was to re-imagine the existing masterplan into a comprehensive interconnected series of dynamic spaces that focus on the programming themes of city's rail/cultural heritage and its relationship with its natural environment.

Construction commenced in May of 2005 and was in final stages of completion as of January 2006. Rocky Point Park now features a central shore side performance stage, innovative grading that channels and naturally cleans stormwater into bio-swales that connect to existing waterways, community art elements found in and around the park and its new train station inspired Public Service Building

Rocky Point Park delineates existing conditions, environmental quality, and regional history, yet it goes beyond a simple retrospective of underutilized community greenspace. The design team delved into the biophysical site, and also into the rich cultural landscape of the greater community. The project scope charged the landscape architects with the responsibility of evaluating the existing park and gathering information related to community attitude, priorities, and program. The final document was to present development scenarios and design themes supported by documentation related to community values.

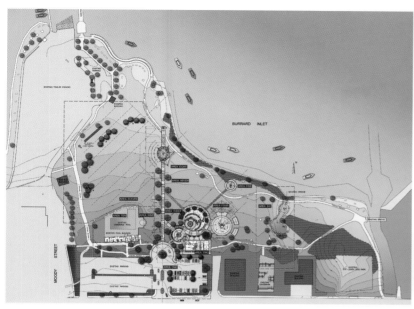

↑   Overall Park masterplan concept.

↗   Water park concept for 'fisherman's 'bobber-balls' – These toys are interactive and were custom manufactured.

↓   Water park in action – all waste water is directed to a bio-filter and back into Burrard Inlet.

← Community scale waterpark with custom water toys that are interactive and user activated. All drainage within this waterpark is directed to a Biofilter before water enters the Ocean Inlet.

↑ Main pedestrian promenade with seating nodes shown in foreground. The main walkway is organized along a railway theme, and the seating areas are metaphorical 'box-cars'.

↓ Entry Plaza for the main park services building —designed as an historic train station.

↙ Typical summer day in the waterpark with the bobber balls in 'full gush'!

↖ Performance stage created to seem like a sailboat on the Inlet.

↑ Adventure playground with a mariner theme.

↗ Pedestrian Pier into Burrard Inlet. Excellent views of the north shore mountains, mudflats and shoreline of the Inlet.

← Entry Planters mark the change in primary to secondary pathways and help visitors find their way through the site.

←← Entry seating modeled after traditional train station benches. Integrated artwork and lighting throughout.

client
City of Port Moody, British Columbia
other key consultants
Architect: e-Atelier architecture, Vancouver;
Engineering: PSTurje and associates;
Engineering: Cobalt engineering
location
Rocky Point Park, Port Moody, British Columbia
completion
Summer 2006
photography
Darren Bernaerdt photography

Forks of the Thames Phase 1 – Civic Plaza & Splash Pad
PMA Landscape Architects Ltd.

The Forks of the Thames is the centerpiece of a revitalization project along the Thames River in downtown London, Ontario. The first phase focuses on the redevelopment of existing passive recreation trail system, into a more engaging active destination with a strong civic identity.

PMA Landscape Architects led the consulting team who developed the overall master plan for the Forks area in 2000. Working closely with the City of London Parks Planning Department, PMA designed a new central waterfront plaza, interactive fountain, and children's splash pad. The City's requirements included retention of an historic residential building and its conversion into an interpretation and information centre, operated by London and Region Art and Historical Museums. Custom signage and interpretive elements were to be integrated into the landscape elements, namely into the feature walls.

Extreme grade changes, accessibility and site views to the river set the parameters for the design of the urban plaza. Tall retaining wall forms the space, while functioning as a massive signage wall and waterfall element. It provides users with an elevated view to the plaza and the river beyond. Visitors to the plaza operate the interactive fountain, while ground jets, waterfalls, spray jets and fibre optic lighting add to the ever-changing waterscape and use of the plaza. A terraced lawn slopes down to the upper terrace punctuated by a custom seatwall with a watertrough running along it, as a symbolic reference to the river.

The most popular summer destination in the area is the interactive splash pad, complete with custom water toys such as a bucket-dump, a "tickle" rail, and various horizontal and vertical jets. The splash pad provides an interactive water play environment for all ages from toddlers to adults alike, as a welcome relief to the summer heat.

awards
2002 – Ontario Concrete Awards Cast-in-Place Award Material Innovation.

→ Planting plan.

↓ Urban plaza with interactive water display.

↓↓ Urban plaza and splash pad.

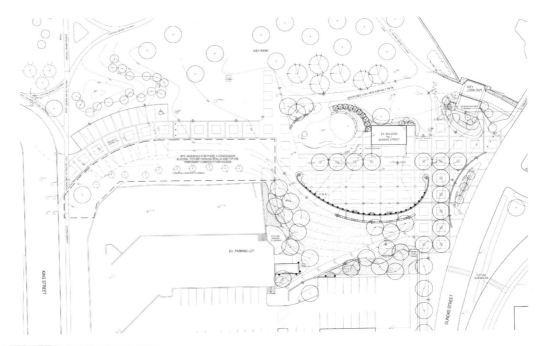

← Urban plaza with historic references on signage, and water features.

→ Interactive water jets and custom mast lighting in urban plaza.

↓ Interactive water jets in urban plaza.

↙ Urban plaza with signage wall, special paving, and water features.

↖ Splash pad at the Forks of the Thames.
→ Custom "tickle" rail at splash pad.
→→ Interactive waterplay equipment.
↓ Splash pad at the Forks of the Thames.
← Seatwall and water jet at splash pad.

← Custom seat wall and water trough on upper terrace.

↑ Architectural trellis at small performance stage.

↗ Custom water trough detail.

→ Watercolour illustration of proposed urban plaza.

client
Corporation of the City of London
location
London, Ontario
other key consultants
Landscape Architect collaborator: Vafiades
  Landscape Architects;
Water feature and splash pad specialist: Rob
  Brogee, Resicom Contracting and Spray Play;
Architect: Natale and Scott Architects;
Civil Engineer: Aquafor Beech Ltd.;
Structural Engineer: Stephenson Engineering Ltd.
completion
Fall 2001
photography
PMA Landscape Architects Ltd.

The Forks Skateable Sculpture Plaza
van der Zalm + associates, Inc.

The Plaza at the Forks is a skateable Sculpture plaza within the heart of downtown Winnipeg, Manitoba, Canada. This plaza is a world-class destination facility for skateboarding and people who appreciate urban art and 'art in motion'. The Plaza at the Forks is the largest and most expansive skate plaza project in North America. The quality of materials, vast terrain (5000m2) and uncompromising attention to detail make this a truly unique urban park for Winnipeg and the rest of Canada. Located at the base of the proposed 'Museum of Human Rights', this plaza enjoys what the 'highest profile' locations within the city and is destined to become a well-known public space for all residents and visitors to the city.

The project has been made possible through the generous donation of over $ 2.5million from the Jim Burns Family Foundation. The notion of the world's first skateable sculpture plaza, garnered immediate support from the donor and the design team set in motion a fast-track process to realize the concept through to construction within a 12 month period. The urban space includes granite capped benches, ledges, stair cases, and flexible performance spaces. Integrated soft landscape and lighting complete the space. Art podiums were integrated throughout the plaza, providing an opportunity for local artists to display their work. Some significant art pieces were built and installed within the park and are also created to be 'used' or skated. Since opening in July of 2006, the Plaza at the Forks has enjoyed international acclaim as the top urban skate plaza in the world. Business development staff from the nearby Forks Marketplace have indicated that tourism has increased as a result of the plaza and they have heard positive comments related to the Plaza from almost everyone who visits. In February 2007, van der Zalm + associates earned a National Honour Award from the Canadian Society of Landscape Architects (CSLA). This project was one of six projects recognized with the nation's highest design honour.

awards
2007 National Honour Award for Design, Canadian Society of Landscape Architects.
"Best use of Public Space": Skaters for Public Skateparks – National Design Award Program

A multi-purpose recreational space that is a skate plaza, an outdoor art gallery, a meeting place, a passive plaza, and a destination spot for the community, a meeting place for all residents - youth, parents, and grandparents. Materials such as stainless steel, acid-etched concrete, unit paver stone and granite create a multi-tactile experience that mimics the urban environment.

The Plaza is a place where one can perform/play or watch/learn; it is a destination, a transition area between the city and the recreational offerings of the Forks development, and spot to watch different groups interact and create innovative experiences. Professional Skateboarders, and amateurs from around North America visited the Forks on opening day.

↑   The quality and attention to detail within the park, and the work of the Landscape Architects to connect the development with the local art community has helped realize the vision of a world class 'inclusive' and fully-integrated development within the waterfront district.

←← "Grinding" the coping within the huge concrete bowl complex.

↖   The "Magic Carpet" – a concrete, acid-etched band that ripples off the Plaza slab and creates a unique art element and skateable feature.

←   The 'port-hole' – viewers are encouraged to monitor park useage from a variety of unique perspectives.

↙   The 'clam-shell' a skateable pool with integrated tile work and lighting.

client
Jim Burns Family Foundation
other key consultants
Local Landscape architect:
  Scatliff+Miller+Murray;
Skatepark Consultant: New Line Skateparks Inc.;
Engineers: KGS Group – Winnipeg
Contractors: PCL Contractors Canada Inc.
  – special projects division.
location
The Forks Marketplace – Winnipeg, Manitoba
completion
July 1st, 2006 (Canada Day)
photography
Mark van der Zalm, Bob Somers, and
  Dwayne Mayze.

Metro Skatepark

LANDinc

While travelling home on their commute from Vancouver Skytrain passengers often comment about the odd concrete shapes of the new skate park the see in Burnaby. While there is another skate park in Burnaby, the designers of this project set themselves apart by choosing environmentally sound building materials, utilizing innovative methods of construction and by engaging the target users of the park throughout the design process. The result is a park that has pushed the development of community skate facilities far forward in terms of professionalism, innovative design, environmental commitment, and community consultation in Canada.

In 2003, Vancouver based LANDinc was hired by the City of Burnaby to design a skate park. Led by landscape architect Jeff Cutler, the firm oversaw public workshops, concept design, design development, working drawings, project management and construction administration. The team also incorporated the expertise of Jim Barnum, a skate park specialist who provided advice on the skateboard specific design of park elements.

From a technical standpoint, the designs of the features in the park are unparalleled. This is the result of LANDinc's commitment to the end users' needs and ideas, as well as from the finish quality of the concrete mix and the masterful workmanship during construction. In this case, the environmental initiative contributed heavily to the quality of the final features.

The regional and national skateboard community in Canada agree that the Metro Skate Park is a very significant project. Other parks often cater to only one kind of skating, or one level of skill. The Metro Skate Park brings three skate styles, all skill levels and a whole lot of enthusiastic youth together in one place, and it is the choice of environmentally sound materials combined with the inclusive, engaging design process that has made the Metro Skate Park so successful and so unique.

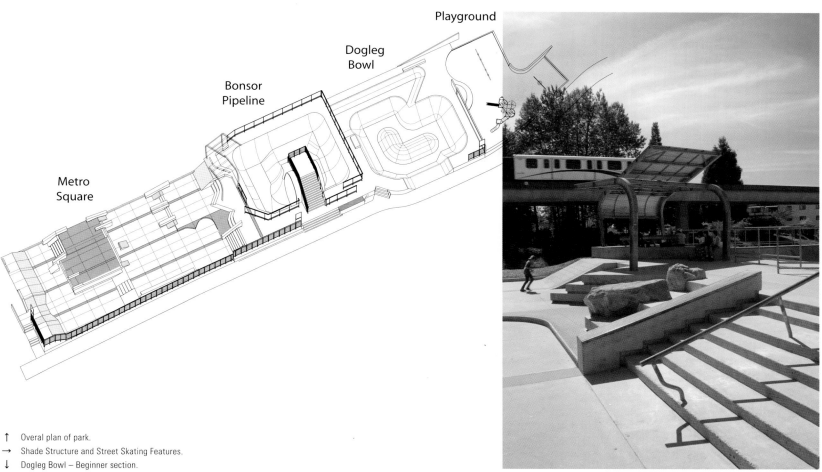

Metro
Square

Bonsor
Pipeline

Dogleg
Bowl

Playground

↑   Overal plan of park.
→   Shade Structure and Street Skating Features.
↓   Dogleg Bowl – Beginner section.

↖ Bonsor Pipeline — Advanced area.

↑ Shade Structure — Hangout area.

← Metro Square — Street Skateboarding area.

client
City of Burnaby
location
Bonsor Park, Burnaby, British Columbia
completion
October 2004
photography
Jeff Cutler

Vancouver Skateplaza – Transforming Under-utilized Urban Spaces

van der Zalm + associates, Inc.

The Vancouver Skateplaza represents a successful urban design that transforms an under-utilized/undesirable urban 'scrap of land' into a unique and dynamic youth facility that aids in rejuvenating an area previously plagued with neglect, drug-abuse, and other crime.

The plaza project serves to: (1.) rejuvenate an under-utilized, irregular shaped urban scrap of land into an efficient, active space that harmonizes with its context (2) provide a unique (and much needed) youth facility/destination for local skateboarders and urban residents, and (3) help re-invigorate a decayed urban area with vitality, spirit, and continuous public presence (to discourage vagrancy and crime, and encourage neighbours to engage in exploring different forms of street culture).

The landscape architects achieved these 3 objectives by bringing together civic, community and interested user groups into a continuous dialogue where all parties were active participants in the design evolution of the facility. The design blends in with its existing context through softscape (matching neighbouring vegetation from Andy Livingstone Park), hardscape (creating an authentic "public plaza" design using materials found in the area [concrete, brick, granite, stainless steel]), and purpose (enhancing the area's already expansive "recreational" facilities).

This project is unique in that an existing 'brown-field' has been rejuvenated both through design, and the presence of people. A plaza dedicated to youth provides an authentic meeting place that helps young people feel valued and contributes to positive urban landmarks within previously marginalized areas of downtown.

↑   Context - Over the course of seven years, local youth activists have tried to create a 'street' plaza facility for both recreation, and socialization. Coupled with this desire was the motivation by the Vancouver Park board to improve an under-utilized site within the downtown core.

↗   The existing site - One 'urban scrap' of under-utilized land in Vancouver is a small triangular site located under the Georgia Street Viaduct along Pacific Boulevard (next to Chinatown, Science World, and the former Expo 86 lands). Once a parking lot, the site was neither successful in this role, nor was it attractive to any potential developers, due to its location directly beneath a busy elevated roadway.

↓   3-d plan perspective - These computer drawings of the new Vancouver Skateplaza. The difficult shape of the site created design challenges: how do you maximize the space of a triangle to produce a multi-use, urban plaza?

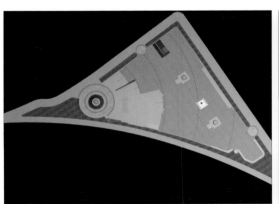
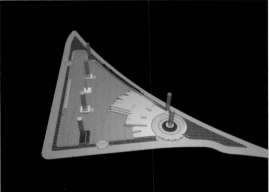
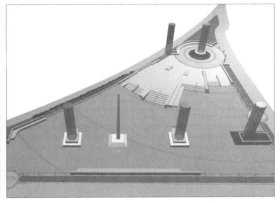
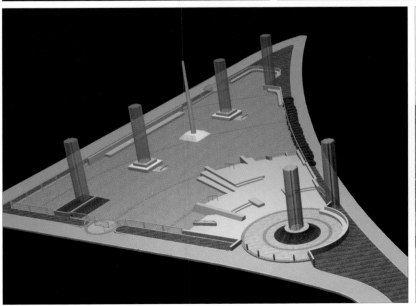

Building the park - By working closely with city officials, neighbours, businesses and local youth, Vancouver Skateplaza has been 'built' with cooperation, understanding and a concern for creating a space that is an active and integrated member of the surrounding community.

New site in action - This photo, shot on the opening day of the plaza shows how quickly the site has become a destination spot for many Vancouverites.

client
City of Vancouver – Park board
other key consultants
Architects: Paul Rust Architects;
Geotechnical Engineers: GeoPacific Engineering;
Structural Engineers: Fast + Epp Engineering;
Aquatic Biologist: Pottinger Ganerty Environmental
  Consultants.
Wildlife Biologist: Ken Summers.
Contractor: New Line Skateparks inc.
team at van der Zalm + associates, Inc.
Mark van der Zalm (project manager, lead
  landscape architect)
Qiang Shan (designer, architect)
Matt Lundin (technician)
Brad Snelling (intern landscape architect, graphic
  design)
location
Vancouvr, BC
completion
Fall – 2004
photography
Mark van der Zalm, Kyle Dion, and the City of
  Vancouver

Residential

Sommets sur le fleuve

WAA

Developed by one of the best developers in Montreal, this living community of four prestigious towers takes full advantage of its breath taking views on the Saint-Laurence River and downtown Montreal. The landscape areas are designed as a series of four private gardens developed around different themes. Indoor and outdoor pools, patios, and diversified theme areas respond to modern living conditions while taking full advantage of the natural settings. Each garden takes full advantage of the unique relationship to the river by providing ample open space for viewing the open water, the reflecting sunrays on the rocky rapids and the fast moving water of the river. Natural plantings along public paths that surround the properties offer a convenient access to an extensive hiking and cycling system, connecting the river to a preserved forest. Two outdoor pools with a pergola and paved terraces provide a unique environment for swimming, reading, and relaxing in a natural setting. Theme areas such as a "zen" garden, a metal gazebo in an apple orchard (reproduced from the Bagatelle Garden in Paris), a butterfly garden, a reflecting pool, and an outside reception space are some of the amenities offered for the pleasure and convenience of the residents.

Developed in a "cul-de sac" or semi crescent street, the four towers form a modern and exciting community with the surrounding mid and low rise. Sculptural glass signage identifies each of the entrances where temporary parking is offered. Except for the visitor's parking located at each of the main entrances, all parking is underground. Lush plantings, floral displays, tree-lined thoroughfares and formal gardens characterize this site's high quality project, where each detail is carefully studied to offer the best living environment for the owners.

Corportation Proment has received many top honour awards for the high construction and design qualities of this unique project.

→ View from the top level on the entrance terrace, between Block 1 and 2, overlooking the outdoor pool area and Zen Garden.

← Entrance terrace and garden overlooking the pool area and the St-Laurence River.

↑ Detail of the Zen Garden.

↓ Building 3 and 4, the Sunken Garden, and the reception area overlooking the reflecting pool and the river.

↙ Entrance terrace overlooking the main entrance and streetscape.

client
Corporation Proment
other key consultants
Jean Pierre Bart, architect
location
Montréal, Québec
completion
2005

550 Queens Quay West
Eguchi Associates Landscape Architects

Reconciling the Flow of Human/ Nature

The site of this condominium landscape is located at Harbourfront in Toronto, Ontario. The primary landscaped area faces Lake Ontario and is located to the south and east of an L-shaped condominium building. The landscape is located above a street level, garage roof slab. In addition to the main building, a small retail pavilion and an adjacent building to the east delineate the overall configuration of the landscape space.

This project is a high-density, residential landscape with typical project constraints such as a restrictive capital budget; rigid, urban design guidelines and many other municipal requirements. City of Toronto guidelines required the inclusion of a north-south, public route through the site and a specific landscape treatment within the public boulevard.

Rather than accepting such factors as limitations that would minimize the possibility of creating a meaningful design, we chose to look at the project as a challenge and an opportunity to investigate the cost-effective development of a landscape that engages people with the spirit of the waterfront. Common materials and construction techniques were therefore used.

Conceptually, the landscape is an attempt to reconcile the human spirit, or the urban/ built environment, with the natural forces that are strongly manifested by the close proximity of Lake Ontario. It is a visually delightful gesture of flowing lines, wavy forms and a challenging mix of materials and elements. It is a metaphor for the healthy realignment of people and environmental processes and one that promotes a visceral engagement leading to real wellness, beauty, harmony and sustainability.

The landscape responds to the flowing balconies of the condominium building. We worked closely with the architect to visually integrate the retail pavilion with the landscape. Together they were designed as a unified whole. The Canada Geese Topiary Frames were included as a reminder that the geese are subjects of environmental concern and controversy at the lakeshore in Toronto.

awards
2003 Regional Honour Award, Canadian Society of Landscape Architects.

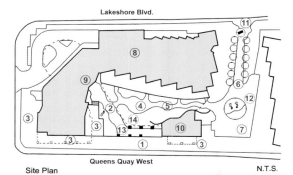

Lakeshore Blvd.

Site Plan   N.T.S.

Queens Quay West

1. Urban Streetscape
2. Residential Entrance Walk
3. Commercial Entrance
4. Semi-Private Garden
5. Meandering Garden Path
6. Undulating Allee
7. Public Plaza

8. L- shaped Building
9. Building Lobby
10. Pavilion
11. Stone Inukshuk
12. Circular 'Island' Planter
    with Canada Geese Topiary Frames
13. Stone Entrance Columns
14. Wavy Metal Fence

↑   Site Plan.

↗   Flowing lines reflect the collaborative journey of the urban environment with natural forces within this organic, linear parterre.

→   Rectilinear patterns embrace curvilinear forms to create meaningful, environmental experiences.

↘   Stone Entrance Columns stand in contrasting harmony with the Urban Streetscape that includes an ordered pattern of steel and concrete building colonnades and trees required by the City of Toronto Streetscape Guidelines for the Harbourfront District.

↓   Indeterminate plant material growth engages unexpectedly with the Stone Entrance Columns.

↑ The wavy Residential Entrance Walk leading to the south entrance of the building lobby includes a playful blend of precast concrete pavers intersecting dramatic drifts of seasonally changing plant material. The Metal Wave Fence encloses the semi-private garden.

↗ The Metal Wave Fence meanders in unique counterpoint with the ornamental grasses and evergreen shrubs during winter months. The fence design is predicated on a repetitive pattern of standard sections with a few heavy steel pickets per panel distributed randomly throughout a standard picket pattern. This has resulted in a cost-effective yet visually active and complex appearance.

↓ The Stone Inukshuk, a traditional native, northern Canadian wayfinding device, stands on guard in a small circular planter and marks the passage south to the water. Asymmetrical, undulating and horizontally misaligned, concrete walls with sandblasted wave patterns intersect and interact with berms and drifts of plantings in counterpoint with the double row of trees of the Undulating Allee.

↑ Drifts of plantings respond to the City of Toronto's requirement for green space adjacent to the street. The Semi-Private Garden includes a rich array of plant species providing a serene setting for the Pavilion, seemingly nestled harmoniously within the landscape. High-cost, custom blue coloured pavers most symbolic of water, were strategically distributed across the site. Natural rocks provide alternatives for seating.

→ The complex dialogue of ornamental grasses whispering to the wind in winter acknowledges the transparency of simple metal features in the landscape.

↙ The Canada Geese Topiary Frames sitting within the circular geometry of the oversized planter, provide sculpture-like qualities to the landscape. Stone seat walls with contrasting rough and smooth-sawn surface textures, provide alternative seating.

← The Meandering Garden Path encourages exploration through drifts of ever-changing plantings.

client
Cenpac Developments Ltd.
project team - eguchi associates
Principal-in-Charge, Real Eguchi, B.A., B.Tech. (Arch.), M.L.Arch., OALA, CSLA
Design Principal, Barbara Flanagan-Eguchi, B.L.Arch., OALA CSLA
Team Members: Juhan Marten, Martin Wade, Eddie Wu, Tad Ukleja, David Ruben Piqtoukun, William Lishman.
other key consultants
Page and Steele Architects Incorporated
Perkins Eastman Black Architects Inc.
Lighting Design: Lightstudio Inc.
location
Toronto, Ontario
completion
2002
photography
bREAL Art + Design

Mississauga Residence

Janet Rosenberg + Associates Landscape Architects Inc.

This private residence in south Mississauga is situated immediately above the Credit River Valley, a significant watershed ravine system in southern Ontario that drains into Lake Ontario. We were retained by the client to provide a master plan for the combined two-lot property that preserved the natural features of the site, primarily the existing woodlot at the back of the property, and provided a variety of garden settings for the client to enjoy.

Our intention was to create a sense of progression from the front of the house to the natural woodland setting at the back of the property. We attempted to achieve this by making the gardens towards the front of the property more formal than the gardens towards the back of the property. The formal gardens were laid out on axial relationships to the house. This allowed us to preserve and protect the existing woodlot, while successfully integrating it with the rest of the property. The overall design for the property includes a formal circular garden at the front of the house, a sunken garden and formal alley at the side of the house, an informal pond and terraces at the back of the house and a woodland trail system at the back of the property.

Our client's love of gardens is reflected in the extensive palette of plant material used throughout the site in lush, horticultural plantings that combine colour, texture and form. The plantings were inspired by traditional Victorian gardens and plants were selected because of their ornamental characteristics as well as their ease of maintenance.

By successfully demonstrating a commitment to the use of traditional design elements, a commitment to quality both in design and implementation and a commitment to detail, we were able to create a beautiful and timeless garden with a variety of settings for our client to enjoy.

↑ Sunken English garden with a profusion of colour.

↘ Lush plantings sit at the forefront of a natural forested area near a ravine.

↓ Finials mark a set of stairs.

↑ The fountain is the focal point of the rose garden with grand beech allee.
↓ The geometry of the garden becomes less formal as it moves towards the ravine's edge.

↑ A rich horticultural tapestry of lush, vibrant plant material demonstrates the continuous evolution and renewal of nature while unifying the physical elements of the site.

↓ View through abundant landscape to pool.

client
Whitfield

other key consultants
Oliveira Landscaping Contractor Ltd.

location
Oakville, Ontario

completion
Rear property July 2001
Front Property July 2005

photography
Neil Fox, Jessie Peterman

Ordered Chaos

A Garden of Harmony, Healing, Diversity and Delight

Eguchi Associates Landscape Architects

This project is the renewal of a diminutive, urban garden located in midtown, Toronto, Ontario.

The client wanted their garden to be imbued with the quality of 'ordered chaos'. Our approach to achieving this request was to utilize a diverse palette or a contrasting yet harmonious mix of materials, forms and processes. We wanted to establish the garden as a refuge of order and sensuous beauty combined with mystery and complexity; a garden where it is apparent that nature and culture easily intermingle. In combining harmony with diversity, we created a haven that engages the human spirit with the healing qualities of the garden.

The layout includes a small, 'ordered' square patio of square-cut limestone located at the bottom of a new metal/wood staircase that was an integral part of the design work. A random limestone path, located to minimize impact to a large existing tree, leads to a garden pavilion and a second, rotated, square sun terrace at the far end of the garden. A secondary path of black, crushed granite quietly meanders beside the oak tree as an alternative journey through the garden.

The project included the design of unique, architectural features that reinforce the theme of 'ordered chaos'. The garden pavilion is a rough-sawn, cedar wood box that floats independently below a glass roof and metal/wood framework. The perimeter fence is constructed of oversized wood members and manifests a sense of security and refuge. Spherical finials, made of refurbished bowling balls, are located randomly and appear to be rolling along the upper fence rail. The new steps connecting to the main floor of the house, constructed of heavy wood planks, contrast with light metal, central stringers and railings and sit daringly on steel rings. A cantilevered wood bench is perched on one of many granite boulders located throughout the garden. Circular/ spherical elements located throughout the garden provide order through repetition.

→ A random-cut, limestone path meanders between a small dining patio and a square, sun terrace within this 7.5 metre wide, urban refuge. The garden pavilion sits adjacent to the rotated, sun terrace of square-cut limestone. A secondary path of crushed granite offers a less ordered and more complex journey through the garden.

The garden promotes a sense of prospect and discovery within its apparent natural randomness while providing comfort within its overall, harmonious composition.

← The garden pavilion is a rough-sawn, cedar wood box that floats independently below a glass roof and metal/wood framework.

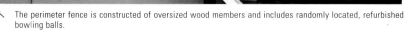 The perimeter fence is constructed of oversized wood members and includes randomly located, refurbished bowling balls.

↑ New steps are constructed of wood and metal and include circular and spherical elements. These motifs are included throughout the garden.

↘ A cantilevered wood bench is perched on one of many granite boulders located throughout the garden. Real Eguchi tests its structural integrity.

← A secondary path of black, crushed granite, quietly meanders beside the oak tree as an alternative journey through the garden.

client
Withheld
project team - eguchi associates
Principal-in-Charge, Real Eguchi, B.A., B.Tech.
 (Arch.), M.L.Arch., OALA, CSLA
Design Principal, Barbara Flanagan-Eguchi,
 B.L.Arch., OALA, CSLA
other key consultants
Structural Engineer: Tony Baggio
location
Midtown Toronto, Ontario
completion
2002
photography
bREAL Art + Design

A Stroll and Sculpture Wellness Garden Sanctuary for Shared Renewal

Eguchi Associates Landscape Architects

This project is the revitalization of a large garden in Toronto, Ontario that we designed and managed over many years. The garden is heavily wooded and steeply sloped.

The project was conceived and master planned as a stroll and sculpture wellness garden. A long series of wide steps was first installed to provide access to the furthest corner of the garden. The limestone staircase meanders between trees and numerous terraces, which were revitalized in phases, to a corner retreat nestled at the bottom of the hill. Smaller restored pathways provide alternate experiences.

The two doctors and their children, who live here, requested a swinging bench in this sunny corner, an essential destination within this overall garden sanctuary that enhances personal and ecological renewal and healing. This latest initiative was to be a place with restorative qualities: a place for reflection, contemplation and conversation.

Our approach was to create a complex yet visually simple overhead structure installed along with sitting walls, sitting rocks, fencing, artwork and plantings. A swinging bench was hung from the structure and oriented, along with a stationary bench, to enhance human contact and views of the overall garden. These were arranged on a stone terrace in a perfect square pattern. Inherent in the square is a sense of order, simplicity and refuge in contrast to the mystery filled, wooded slope that one passes through to reach this quiet corner.

Our belief is that in combining order with diversity, we create a landscape that engages the human spirit with the healing qualities of the garden.

The materials used throughout the garden are many and different and reflect this approach, yet they are combined in a manner that feels unified and whole. Wood, stone and metal in many shapes and patterns, are carefully crafted and composed along with a diverse range of plant materials. Sculpture animates the corner terrace and is placed engagingly throughout the garden.

↑ A swinging bench hangs from a garden
   structure, alongside a stationary bench,
   and is oriented to enhance human
   contact and views of the overall garden.
   These were arranged on a square, stone
   terrace.

→ A wood fence of random-sized boards
   is combined to contrast with wood
   screens with their more orderly, square,
   openings.

→→ An intermittent stone wall is combined
   with evergreen and deciduous shrubs to
   provide visual layering to complement
   the wood fence and screens.

↑ A Japanese stone lantern is a vertical focal point that animates this upper level, grass terrace.

↗ An upper level patio, embellished with flowerpots, commences the journey down into the garden.

↓ A perennial and annual flowerbed provides sanctuary for a sculpture of Peter Pan by artist Ken Nice. The bronze figure floats joyfully above the garden and alongside a Japanese maple and the stump of an old tree.

↖ A partial view of the long, stone staircase that was first installed to provide access to the furthest corner of the garden.

↑ A sculptural 'Snakes and Ladders', metal guardrail created by artist Ron Baird, intermingles with vines.

↓ A custom metal, post bracket supports one wood column of the swinging bench structure. The adjacent rusting steel, garden edging is another use of metal in the garden.

← A sculpture created by artist E. B. Cox is a playful, engaging focal point located at the end of a narrow, grass terrace.

client
Withheld
project team - eguchi associates
Principal-in-Charge, Real Eguchi, B.A., B.Tech.
  (Arch.), M.L.Arch., OALA, CSLA
Design Principal, Barbara Flanagan-Eguchi,
  B.L.Arch., OALA, CSLA
other key consultants
Structural Engineer: Tony Baggio
location
Baby Point, Toronto, Ontario
completion
2004
photography
bREAL Art + Design

Toronto Waterfront Terrace

Janet Rosenberg + Associates Landscape Architects Inc.

Inspired by the scenic lakeside setting of this penthouse terrace, a unique symphony of materials was blended to complement and harmonize with the natural elements of wind, sunlight and water.

The contemporary design features a hand carved Indiana stone bowl fountain and serpentine steel wall on the south terrace. This interesting juxtaposition of smooth steel and textured stone creates some diversity in the sensory context.

A linear stone water trough on the west terrace mitigates sound from the adjacent freeway, and ornamental grasses provide texture and movement while instilling a sense of privacy.

↖ Inspired by the scenic lakeside setting of this penthouse terrace, a unique symphony of materials are juxtaposed to compliment and natural elements of sunlight, wind and water.

↑ A water feature is a focal point, composed of steel, textural stone, with a carved Indiana limestone basin.

↘ Unique water trough links the different areas of the terrace.

↓ Textural detail of steel and pebbles.

← Graceful plumes of grasses play on the quality of light on the terrace.

client
Withheld
other key consultants
Oliveira Landscaping Contractor Ltd.
Prototype Design Lab
Dan Euser Waterarchitecture Inc. (DEW)
location
Toronto, Ontario
completion
July 2001
photography
Sharon Kish

– 263 –

Company Profile

architectsAlliance

205-317 Adelaide St West, Toronto, Ont., CAN
M5V-1P9
T: +1 416-593-6500   F: +1 416-593-4911
adicastri@architectsalliance.com
www.architectsalliance.com
Adrian DiCastri, partner
Peter Clewes, partner
Walter Bettio, project architect
Deni Papetti, project architect

Behnisch Architekten

Rotebühlstraße 163A, Stuttgart, 70197 Germany
T: +(49) 711-607-72-0   F: +(49) 711-607-72-99
stb@behnisch.com
www.behnisch.com
Stefan Behnisch, parnter
Volker Biermann, project architect

Diana Gerrard Landscape Architecture

67 Stanley Avenue, Hawkestone, Ontario L0L 1T0
T: +1 705-487-6438
dianagerrardla@rogers.com
Diana Gerrard, principal

du Toit Allsopp Hillier

Add: 50 Park Road Toronto, Ontario, M5E 1P8,
Canada
T: +1 416-968-9479   F: +1 416 968 0687
admin@dtah,com
www.dtah.com
Gillian Nasmith

architectsAlliance (aA) was founded in 1999 by Peter Clewes, Adrian DiCastri and John van Nostrand. aA is known for its sophisticated and urbane approach to high-density development, and for creating innovative reinterpretations of conventional building types through a diverse range of projects. Recent projects include the Pond Road Student Residence at York University; the LEED-qualified Kaiser Engineering Building, at the University of British Columbia; the expansion and renovation of the Canadian Chancery in The Hague, the Netherlands; mixed residential/commercial projects in Cambridge, MA; Minneapolis, MN; and Nijmegen, the Netherlands.

Behnisch Architekten founded in 1989 under the name Behnisch, Behnisch & Partner is a renowned full-service practice with a distinguished history. Stefan Behnisch is partner of both Stuttgart, Germany, and Venice, California, USA, offices. He is joined in Stuttgart by partners Martin Haas and David Cook, and in California—where the firm is known as Behnisch Architects—by partner Christof Jantzen, AIA. The firm is a leader in creating distinctive architectural solutions that are environmentally sustainable. Its achievements have been honored by prestigious award programs, such as Royal Institute of British Architects, Chicago Athenaeum, Holcim Award, and AIA COTE, among others. Notable projects include the platinum-LEED-rated Genzyme Center in Cambridge, MA; Norddeutsche Landesbank (Nord LB) in Hanover, Germany; The St. Benno Grammar School in Dresden, Germany; Mill Street Lofts in Los Angeles; and the Institute for Forestry and Nature Research in Wageningen, The Netherlands. The firm works in both the public and private sectors and has an excellent record in architectural competitions, where the majority of its commissions are gained.

Exploring the relationship between nature and culture, Diana Gerrard Landscape Architecture (DGLA) challenges traditional concepts of design. DGLA's work results from knowledge of history and tradition, sympathy with contemporary needs, understanding of both conceptual and material processes, mastery of construction, and attention to detail. From defining the program to forming the space and experimenting with materials, DGLA has developed expertise with all of the components, tools and processes of landscape architecture at a broad range of scales. Representative projects include Canadian Centre for Architecture in Montreal; Ashbridges Bay Treatment Plant Site Design, Alliance Francaise, Canadian Opera Company, and Bronfman Residence in Toronto; and Four Seasons Hotels Executive Headquarters in Don Mills, Ontario.

du Toit Allsopp Hillier is one of the few Canadian multi-discipline design firms that, for many years has embraced urban design as its central, integrative discipline. Established in 1975, the firm of 24 is comprised of planners, architects and landscape architects with six principals who maintain direct and continuing involvement through all phases of the work. The firm has been highly influential in contributing to the urban design vision and urban landscape design for Canada's National Capital Parliamentary Precinct in Ottawa for which they have received both national and international recognition. Other areas of expertise include urban renewal, transportation related urban design, bridge architecture and campus planning and design. In each of these areas the firm has establish a strong reputation for both planning and implemented work. Together with West 8 of Rotterdam, the firm has recently won an international design competition for the public realm design of Toronto's central waterfront.

Ecosign Mountain Resort Planners Ltd.

8073 Timber Lane, PO Box 63, Whistler BC, V0N
1B0, Canada
T: +1 604-932-5976   F: +1 605-932-1897
info@ecosign.com
www.ecosign.com
Don Murray (dmurray@ecosign.com)

Full Service Planning and Landscape Architecture
firm specializing in the design of Mountain
Resort Communities and Recreational Facilities
Worldwide.

Eguchi Associates Landscape Architects

(A Division of Design With Nature Incorporated)

Add: 39 Ferris Road, Toronto, Ontario M4B 1G2,
Canada
T: +1 416-759-7529   F: +1 416-759-5078
real@bREAL.ca
www.bREAL.ca
Real Eguchi

Eguchi Associates Landscape Architects has
provided a complete range of professional landscape
architectural services since 1989. Together with
bREAL Art + Design, a related company, our current
combined portfolio of work includes a broad range
of Canadian and international planning, landscape
architecture and environmental art projects.

Mission
Our primary focus is the enhancement of people's
lives by promoting wellness and beauty. We strive to
achieve this in balance with healthy environments,
both natural and designed. We promote a sustainable,
wonder-filled relationship between people and their
place through landscape, art and design.

Our mission is to design places that allow for the
exploration and revelation of nature, places that
encourage people to be themselves, to be real. On
a regular basis, we want people to embrace and be
joyfully engaged with nature's processes. Visceral
pleasure, sensuous delight, mystery and intrigue,
as well as prospect and refuge, are important
experiential elements to be balanced in a harmonious
and synergistic whole.

Philosophy
It is our strong belief that wellness and beauty
are enhanced with the consistent and revelatory
engagement of people and natural processes
within their immediate environment. Meaningful
interaction increases respect for nature and this
leads to sustainable lifestyles. Designed places
must be restorative and sustaining for individuals,
communities and the environment. Human needs
balanced with nature's ability to sustain us results
in a reconciliatory, healing relationship. We call
this shared renewal. This is ecological and it is
imperative to sustainable design. Sustainable design
acknowledges the complexity and ever-changing
qualities and character of nature and the harmony and
beauty within nature that must be revealed.

Well-designed landscapes, beautiful places, help
to promote and preserve community spirit, which
contributes to our well-being. Civic pride and
positive human interaction are critical considerations
in the design of the constructed environment.
The relationship between people and place is
complex and we must provide for its harmonious
expression.

The aesthetic of a place emerges through our
design exploration and the associated visuals and
other sensory techniques we use to express ideas,
observations and relationships. There is difference
and a creative tension that is found between order
and chaos and this leads to the search for unity
in the differences inherent to every project and
situation. Unity is to be discovered and created
within diversity.

Design Process
We involve people in our design process, which is
really a journey of emotional, intellectual and spiritual
engagement, discovery and resolution leading to
a unified vision and outcome. Our expectation is
that this process continues on well after our work
is complete. Our design process is grounded in real
experience, real beauty and continued growth. We
have learned much but our learning is ongoing. We
act with humility and treat people and environments
with respect. Our challenge in design is not in applying
what we know already; it is in discovering what we
do not yet know about people and their places. We
strive to expose and express the uniqueness of every
project in a manner that contributes to the well-being
of individuals and communities through the creation
of health-full, beautiful places.

**Janet Rosenberg + Associates Landscape
Architects Inc.**

Add: 148 Kenwood Ave, Toronto, Ontario, Canada
M6C 2S3
T: +1 416-656-6665   F: +1 416-656-5756
office@jrala.ca
www.jrala.ca
Janet Rosenberg

Janet Rosenberg + Associates provides a full range of
professional landscape architectural services, offering
innovative master planning, high quality detail design,
and thorough project management. Established in
1983, the firm's portfolio of work includes master
plans, university campuses, institutional facilities,
urban parks, streetscapes, condominiums, rooftop
terraces and green roofs, residential gardens and
estates, botanical gardens, and historical landscape
restorations.

The firm seeks to explore the construction of new
spatial systems which provide seamless connections
between built forms and the natural environment.
Working with the architecture and existing conditions,
JRA develops a holistic and sustainable urban
program for each site. New circulation systems and
layered spaces provide opportunities for flexible
and diverse outdoor activities, cultural events and
mixed use urban development.   JRA seeks to
articulate the complex systems of the public realm
and natural environment, providing fluid transitions
and interactions which improve the experience and
quality of daily life.

The firm is committed to a team approach for each
project, working in close conjunction with clients
and consultants, to provide quality design ranging
from classical to contemporary. Janet Rosenberg,
the principal, maintains an active involvement in
every project and contributes her exceptional detail
resolution and sound technical expertise to each
design. A strong project management organizational
system is utilized to control schedule, budget and
quality assurance on all projects. Dedicated to the
highest quality planting design, the firm is unique
in employing certified horticulturists in addition to
landscape architects.

LANDinc
309-318 Homer Street Vancouver, British Columbia
V6B 2V2, Canada
T: +1 604-646-4110   F: +1 604-646-4120
vancouver@landinc.ca
www.landinc.ca
Jeff Cutler

#409 - 224 Wallace Ave. Toronto, Ontario M6H
1V7, Canada
T: +1 416-657-8881   F: +1 416-352-5201
toronto@landinc.ca

1 Starr Lane Dartmouth, Nova Scotia B2Y 4V7,
Canada
T: +1 902-61-2525   F: +1-902-465-3131
Halifax@landinc.ca

PMA Landscape Architects Ltd.
224 Wallace Avenue, Suite 321
Toronto, Ontario, M6H 1V7 , Canada
T: +1 416-239-9818   F: +1 416-239-1310
design@pmalarch.ca
www.pmalarch.ca
James Melvin

PWL Partnership Landscape Architects Inc.
Add: 5th Floor, East Asiatic House, 1201 West
Pender, Vancouver, British Columbia V6E 2V2.
Canada
T: +1 604-688-6111   F: +1 604-688-6112
pwl@pwlpartnership.com
www.pwlpartnership.com
Bruce Hemstock

The design team of Janet Rosenberg + Associates utilizes various design and illustration techniques, ranging from conventional hand drawings and physical models to sophisticated digital three-dimensional renderings, for design development and presentation drawings. The office is fully equipped with the computing infrastructure required for the efficient preparation and delivery of contract documentation.

Janet Rosenberg + Associates have been honoured with over 80 awards for their work. This includes several design awards from the Canadian Society of Landscape Architects and the Design Exchange. Most recently the firm has won first place in the following design competitions; HtO: Toronto Harbourfront Parks and Open Space System competition, Winnipeg City Crossing Design competition and Landmark: Markham City Centre competition.

LANDinc. is a multi-disciplinary design firm with offices in Vancouver, Toronto and Halifax.

We apply our collective expertise in urban design, environmental planning, sustainable infrastructure, information graphics and landscape architecture to a wide range of private and public sector projects throughout Canada and internationally.

PMA Landscape Architects Ltd. is an award-winning Canadian landscape architectural firm based in Toronto, Ontario that provides complete planning and design services for projects in the public and private realm.

PMA was founded in 1982, and has developed a reputation based on the different, yet complementary skills and strengths of principals James Melvin and Rudolf Hofer, and associate Fung Lee. The firm has earned a reputation as a creative design firm with professional integrity, technical knowledge, and environmental ethic. The studio has consistently maintained a manageable size of seven landscape architects and designers to ensure these attributes remain at their highest level.

PMA enjoys working on projects that pursue best practices in terms of designing for play, sustainability, and civic realm. It has won numerous awards from professional peer organizations such as the Canadian Society of Landscape Architects, and most recently from the Design Exchange of Toronto for Best Landscape Architecture for the project Toronto Botanical Garden in 2006.

PWL Partnership Landscape Architects Inc. is a landscape architectural firm with over thirty years of experience in the planning and design of public and private open space. Our depth of expertise and professionalism in British Columbia has afforded us the opportunity to practice our skills in other parts of Canada, the United States, as well as China, Portugal and Malaysia.

PWL Partnership's design philosophy draws inspiration from the ecological, historical and cultural aspects of the landscape to produce designs that are innovative, imaginative, sustainable, distinct, appropriate, and cost effective. We attempt to reflect the natural and cultural history of an area in our development of public places. If such references can stir even the slightest curiosity, then a connection is made between the site and the visitor. Such connections turn anonymous sites into memorable places that recognize the local vernacular.

PWL Partnership has a staff of twenty-five, which include four principals, a number of senior staff, Landscape Architects, two LEED™ Accredited Professionals and a Certified Arborist.

Scott Torrance Landscape Architect Inc.
26C Dingwall Avenue, Toronto, Ontario, Canada
T: +1 416-469-4343   F: +1 416-463-9119
storrance@sympatico.ca
www.scotttorrance.ca
Scott Torrance

Stoss Landscape Urbanism
51 Melcher Street, suite 601, Boston, MA 02210,
USA
T: +1 617-832-0660   F: +1 617-832-0670
cr@stoss.net
www.stoss.net
Chris Reed

SWA Group
2200 Bridgeway Boulevard, Post Office Box 5904,
Sausalito, California, USA
T: +1 415-332-5100   F: +1 415-332-0719
sausalito@swagroup.com
www.swagroup.com

Scott Torrance Landscape Architect Inc., is a client-focused practice dedicated to providing the highest in client service and design excellence in the public, private and corporate sector.

Stoss is a critical, collaborative design and planning studio that operates at the juncture of landscape architecture, urban design, and planning—in an emerging field known as landscape urbanism. This field addresses sites in relation to the broader ecological, environmental, infrastructural, and social-cultural processes and systems that constitute them; it understands sites as caught up in the landscape process and civic life. As a professional practice, Stoss is unique in the ways it looks to bring these issues to bear in the design of new open spaces and in the framing of civic, institutional, and landscape strategies.

Founded in 2000, Stoss traces its roots to 1995 with the design and exhibition of a number of landscape urbanism projects, early studies in strategic framework planning, brownfields recovery, and stormwater harvesting. Since then, the studio has won national and international recognition for landscape projects rooted in infrastructure, functionality, and ecology. Projects have been published in the Landscape Urbanism Reader; a forthcoming book by Birkhauser Verlag, 306090-09; Architecture; Landscape Architecture; Metropolis; ArchitectureBoston; PRAXIS 4; and Land Forum 13.

Stoss is an intentionally small studio; we bring a high level of energy and commitment to each project. We have the ability, time, and motivation to work closely with clients and teams to fully understand and develop individual project goals and demands, thereby embarking on a process of design and discovery that is both responsive and catalytic. Yet our practice is networked to other design and engineering firms; to experts in academia that are advancing the fields of ecology and urbanism; and to research centers conducting field experiments in emerging brownfields technologies, for instance. Parts of these coalitions coalesce, formally or informally, as specific projects demand; they allow us to both expand resources and tailor expertise to the issues at hand. And they form the basis for imaginative and multi-disciplinary collaborations that better address the complexities of contemporary projects.

CHRIS REED is the founding principal of Stoss. He holds an AB cum laude in Urban Studies from Harvard College and an MLA from the University of Pennsylvania. Reed is a lecturer at the University of Pennsylvania and is currently teaching at the University of Toronto. He is a Research Fellow in the Center for Technology and Environment at the Harvard Design School and a Lecturer at the University of Pennsylvania. Prior to founding Stoss, he worked for six years at Hargreaves Associates on large- and small-scale public and institutional planning and design projects, including the Clinton Presidential Library and Waterfront Park in Little Rock; Waterfront Park in Louisville; and various civic plazas and gathering spaces at the University of Cincinnati. Reed is a licensed landscape architect. He lectures nationally and internationally and is published in several recent works on landscape urbanism and brownfields recovery.

For over 45 years, SWA Group has been recognized as one of the world's leaders in the fields of landscape architecture, planning and urban design. Our projects have received over 450 awards, been showcased in 47 states and more than 40 countries, and our principals are acknowledged as among the industry's most talented and experienced designers and planners. After emerging in 1959 as West Coast office of Sasaki, Walker and Associates, the firm first assumed the SWA Group name in 1975.

Although one of the largest firms of its size in the world, SWA is organized into smaller studio-based offices. These offices enhance creativity and are attuned to client response. Historically, over 75% of our work has come from repeat clients. In addition to bringing strong aesthetic, functional, and social design ideas to our projects, we are also committed to integrating principles of environmental sustainability. At the core of our work is a passion for imaginative, solution-oriented design that adds value to land, buildings, cities, regions and people's lives.

Thib Studio

64 Condor Ave., Toronto, Ontario M4J 3M9,
Canada

T: +1 416-461-8027   F: +1 416-461-8027

jetbah@interlog.com

Jeannie Thib

Tom Barratt Ltd.

Add: 8605 Drifter Way, Whistler, BC V0N 1B8,
Canada

T: +1 604-932-3040   F: +1 604-932-8959

tom@tblla.com

www.tblla.com

Tom Barratt

van der Zalm + associates inc.

suite 2200, 1177 W. Hastings St., Vancouver,
British Columbia, Canada - V3E 2K3

T: +1 604-882-0024   F: +1 604-882-0042

mark@vdz.ca

www.vdz.ca

Mark van der Zalm

Ruoy Chai International Building
Suite 806, No. 8 Yongandongli, Jianguomenwai,
Chaoyang District, Beijing City, PR China

T: +86 10 8528-9498   F: +86 10 8528-9508

Ziang Shan (Design Director)

Vertechs Design Inc.

1200 Bay Street, Suite 803, Toronto, Ontario M5R
2A5, Canada

T: +1 416-925-6097   F: +1 416-925-1782

office@vertechsdesign.com

www.vertechsdesign.com

Mary Jane Lovering

Jeannie Thib is a visual artist producing indoor and outdoor public art and gallery works. Recent public projects include MOTH Gardens, Downsview Memorial Parkette, Toronto, Canada, with Landscape Architect Scott Torrance, commissioned by the City of Toronto, an exterior glass frit design for the Esplanade Arts and Heritage Centre, Medicine Hat, Alberta, Canada, commissioned by the City of Medicine Hat (Diamond and Schmitt Architects) and "The Cranes: A National Tribute to Japanese Canadian Life", an interior slate and maple wall installation commissioned by the Japanese Canadian Cultural Centre, Toronto, (KPMB Architects). Thib's work has been exhibited internationally and is represented in numerous public and private collections including The National Gallery of Canada, Musée des Beaux-Arts de Montréal, Quebec and The Washington DC Convention Center, USA.

Tom Barratt Ltd. stands out as a leading firm in resort development, graphic and digital illustration and design skills.

We are able to provide a comprehensive multimedia digital methodology to each project. Tom Barratt Ltd. recently won awards for the 2010 Winter Olympic Bid and a Whistler Village enhancement project.

The firm has undertaken commissions for landscape design, resort planning, digital graphic production on a wide range and size of projects.

van der Zalm + associates inc. (vdz) is a full service Landscape Architecture and Development consulting firm with offices in British Columbia , Alberta and Ontario.

Established at the turn of the millennium, vdz employs experienced, qualified, and registered professionals with a passion for their work. Our focus is Parks and Recreation. We enjoy a strong national reputation for our work in developing action sports facilities – skatepark, bmx, and technical mountain bike. We also work closely with communities to develop masterplans, urban parks, streetscape plans, water parks, and environmental projects.

We ensure that each development project, be it micro or macro in scale, receives focused attention to detail until completion. Our reputation is growing with projects throughout Canada, the United States, and Europe.

Vertechs Design Inc. was established in 1981. The principals, Mary Jane Lovering, Dip.P.T., B.L.A., and Inese Bite, B.L.A. have a wide range of experience working on diverse project types. These include research, recreational settings, children's play environments, housing developments, educational facilities and healthcare settings including long term care, acute care, chronic care and rehabilitation and palliative care.

Expertise has been established in the traditional areas of landscape architectural design and construction. The firm's experience is augmented by a strong understanding of the particular issues related to site planning, programme requirements, safety and security issues, accessibility, budget constraints, maintenance and microclimate issues. Although each project is addressed on an individual basis these concepts over all are applied in an economical and practical approach for each design problem.

Vertechs Design Inc. has spent considerable energy researching issues related to environmental sustainability. These principles are routinely applied throughout the conceptualization and detail development of the site. Mary Jane Lovering is a LEEDTM Accredited Professional.

The principals have a combination of education in the fields of physiotherapy, gerontology and landscape architecture. With this background and experience, Vertechs Design Inc. is particularly well-suited and committed to providing specialized programming and